PROJECT MANAGEMENT
SURVIVAL

MORE PRAISE FOR
PROJECT MANAGEMENT SURVIVAL

"Recommended for anyone who ever needs to manage a project
– which means anyone who needs to make something happen."
Rupert Baines, Vice President, picoChip

"You know a book is good when you start reading common sense.
This one gives Project Managers tools and answers that are re-
freshingly clear and free of jargon."
Simon Over, major civil engineering project manager,
Dubai Consultancy

"With clarity, Richard Jones's magnus opus on project
management offers the best alternative for explaining the tools
and techniques used in handling real-time, complex projects."
Ghassan Ali Murad, Senior Manager, Batelco

"Contains wonderful real-life scenarios with the type of solution
that always invokes a 'why didn't I think of that' reaction.
A great resource."
Abdulrahman Mutrib, Chief Operations Officer of
Atheeb Communications

"This book should be compulsory reading for all involved in
projects – read it, keep it handy for reference and then recommend
it to your friends and colleagues."
Brett Watson, Former CEO of BT plc Company

PROJECT MANAGEMENT SURVIVAL

A practical guide to leading, managing & delivering challenging projects

RICHARD JONES

KOGAN PAGE

London and Philadelphia

First published in Great Britain and the United States in 2007 by Kogan Page Limited

120 Pentonville Road
London N1 9JN
United Kingdom
www.kogan-page.co.uk

525 South 4th Street, #241
Philadelphia PA 19147
USA

© Richard Jones, 2007

The right of Richard Jones to be identified as the author of this work has been asserted by him in accordance with the Copyright, Designs and Patents Act 1988.

ISBN-13   978 0 7494 5010 6

British Library Cataloguing-in-Publication Data

A CIP record for this book is available from the British Library.

Library of Congress Cataloging-in-Publication Data

Jones, Richard, 1964–
    Project management survival : a practical guide to leading, managing and delivering challenging projects / Richard Jones. – 1st ed.
        p. cm.
    Includes bibliographical references.
    ISBN-13: 978-0-7494-5010-6
    ISBN-10: 0-7494-5010-X
  1. Project management. 2. Teams in the workplace–Management. I. Title.
    HD69.P75J664 2007
    658.4'04–dc22

                                                           2007017736

Typeset by JS Typesetting Ltd, Porthcawl, Mid Glamorgan
Printed and bound in Great Britain by MPG Books Ltd, Bodmin, Cornwall

Contents

Acknowledgements   *ix*

Introduction   1

Part I. Understanding Projects

1. **What Are Projects and Why Do They Fail?**   5
    What is a project? 5; What is project management? 6;
    Why is it vital to manage projects well? 8; Project
    killers 9

2. **Dead Project Walking – Why some projects must be
    killed**   13
    Why dead projects live on 14

Part II. Where are We?

3. **Diagnosing an Existing Project**   19
    Why doing a diagnostic makes sense 19; Getting to the
    truth 20; Digging into the plan 24; Diagnosing a multi-
    company programme 28

Part III. Getting the Right Initial Plan

4. **Leading Projects**   **33**
   The wrong kind of project managers 33; Being the
   right kind of project manager 34; Give the team
   responsibility 35; Managing in a matrix 36; Being a
   team player 37; Overcoming 'It can't be done' 38;
   Focusing your attention in the right places 41

5. **Project Scope and Initiation**   **44**
   Introduction 44; Project initiation 45; The Project
   Charter 48; Creating the Project Charter 48; Get it right
   early on – it's cheaper 50; Summary and actions 56

6. **Agreeing Objectives**   **57**
   Why objectives are important 57; Developing well-
   defined objectives 59; Good and bad objectives – some
   examples 61; Summary and actions 65

7. **Milestones**   **66**
   The problem with bad milestones 67; How to write a
   good milestone 68; Writing milestones 70; Differences
   between milestones and gates 70; Summary and
   actions 74

8. **Refining Milestones**   **76**
   Do you have the right milestones? 76; How result paths
   help 76; Setting up result paths 77; Assessing result
   paths 79; Developing the detail for each milestone 82;
   Beyond milestones 82; Summary and actions 83

9. **Activities/Work Breakdown Structure**   **85**
   What is a work breakdown structure? 86; The
   work breakdown structure underpins much of the
   planning 89; The rolling wave approach 90; The impact
   of rolling wave on estimation and contingency 91;
   Summary and actions 93

10. **Assigning Resources**   **96**
    Identifying the resources you need 96; Summary and
    actions 98

11. Time Estimation   **100**

Why estimation goes wrong 100; Why managing
using 'percentage complete' doesn't work 102; A better
approach for estimation – work content 106; Producing
good estimates 108; Record any assumptions used in
estimation 111; Summary and actions 112

12. Resource Availability   **114**

Estimating task durations from the work content 114;
Summary and actions 122

13. Dependencies   **124**

Different types of dependencies 125; Lag 126;
Predecessors and successors 128; Tasks and sub-
tasks 129; Critical path 131; Slack/float 133; Summary
and actions 134

14. Risk and Mitigation   **136**

The problems with simple risk/contingency
planning 137; Identifying and managing risks 137;
Risk identification 138; Risk assessment 139; Risk
reduction 143; Risk management 145; Summary and
actions 146

Part IV. Getting the Plan Right

15. Optimizing the Plan   **151**

Create more realistic resource usage 152; Improve
resource usage to shorten the duration of key tasks 153;
Reducing task durations on the critical path 157; Working
in parallel 157; Optimization and risk 158; Project
crashing 160; Developing the project budget 163;
Where you end up is where you start 163

Part V. Staying on Track

16. Roles, Responsibilities and Communication   **167**

Project manager 167; Work package or module
managers 169; Project team members 169; Project
sponsor 170; Project office 171; Steering group 171;
Communication between the roles 172; Project
manager's weekly checklist 175

17. **Updating the Plan**   **178**
The update information you need from team
members 178; Integrating the updates 179; Updating
the plan in practice 181; How often? 182

18. **Monitoring Progress**   **183**
Introduction 183; How to monitor progress within a
project 184; Earned Value Analysis (EVA) 186; Using
EVA to monitor progress 190; Limitations of EVA 193

19. **Handling Issues**   **194**
Introduction 194; What is an issue? 195; Prioritizing
issues 195; Managing issues 195

20. **Controlling Change**   **197**

21. **Reporting**   **201**
Reporting down 201; Reporting up 202

22. **Project Closure**   **203**

Appendix 1: The Changing Nature of Projects   *205*
Appendix 2: Project Management Software   *211*
Appendix 3: Project Management Approaches and
    Methodologies   *219*
Appendix 4: Problem-solving Techniques   *229*
Appendix 5: References and Resources   *233*

Index   *235*

Acknowledgements

A very big thank you to the many project teams and major programmes I've worked with over the years. Your patience, questions, good humour and hard work have helped me learn what works and what doesn't.

I'd like to thank my close friends and partners Stefan Stanislawski and Mikael Sandberg for their support. You guys are the best in the business and help make Ventura Team LLP a fantastic company (www.venturateam.com).

My thanks to my great friend Dr Peter Allen (www.nu-angle.com) and my buddy Dr Alaric Naiman (www.transitionstates.com). Working with these guys showed me what being world class at what you do means in action. They have introduced innovative new approaches that turn project management into true project leadership.

Thanks to Rob Morland for watching my back when I first started turning projects around.

Thank you to my sisters Sue and Maura for their constant encouragement and support.

My love and thanks to Julie and great little boys Harry and PJ for believing daddy can do anything and giving me the time and space to write this book.

Finally thank you to my late parents – for making everything possible.

Introduction

Imagine this scenario. You have been asked to take over your company's most important project. Senior management are very upbeat about everything and appear confident in your ability to bring the project in on time and budget. There's a lot riding on your shoulders.

On digging into the project, you find that the main deliverables to date appear to be two-inch thick piles of project plans and you can't find anyone who really appears to know what is happening. You start to get that uneasy feeling that maybe the printer is spewing CVs and you have actually taken on a nightmare of a project. This book is for you and for those about to take on a tough new project.

This book is about successfully managing *real* projects. I don't mean those nice, neat projects where you can hand-pick the team members, where you never have problems with management and where everything goes right. Personally I've never seen one of those, but I've seen far too many project management books that assume the odds are stacked in your favour. This book doesn't! It deals with what to do when you start or inherit projects where resources are scarce, time is short and things may already be going wrong. It takes a pragmatic but highly effective approach to how to succeed in the toughest project situations. It may save your job or even make your whole career!

GETTING STARTED

This book is divided into five parts, which take you from diagnosing the state of an existing project through to creating a realistic new project plan and then maintaining it during the life of the project.

Part I – Understanding Projects
This will help you learn about projects, why they can go so badly wrong and what to look out for in real life.

Part II – Where are We?
This section shows you how to quickly diagnose problems in an existing project that you've taken over – or that you need to assess. It explains how to get beneath the surface of the project and get to the true situation fast.

Part III – Getting the Right Initial Plan
This section shows you how to start a new project from scratch or rebuild a troubled existing project. At the end of the section you will have an initial version of the plan that you can then go on to optimize in Part IV.

Part IV – Getting the Plan Right
This part will help you create a realistic and optimized plan that you can then use to manage the project.

Part V – Staying on Track
Having produced a realistic project plan at the start of the project, this section explains how to manage the project team to ensure you have the right information to make decisions and update the plan to reflect the changing situation over time. It will help you highlight issues early and resolve them before they become crises.

If you want to learn about the full range of issues in project management then I recommend you read the book from the start. If you're taking over an existing project, you can start with Part II. If you're starting a new project you can go straight to Part III. If you are short of time you can start the book where it is closest to your current situation.

Part I

Understanding Projects

1

What Are Projects and Why Do They Fail?

Let's start at the beginning and quickly build up an understanding of what projects are meant to be and how they frequently go wrong.

WHAT IS A PROJECT?

There are some characteristics that hold true for all projects – good and bad.

A project has a temporary organization

This means that the group of people working on the project, whether full or part time, have been brought together to execute the project and will not exist as a team beyond it. This is true even if the project has a duration running into years. For example, the people building the Channel Tunnel that links England and France were brought together for this epic project and the team dispersed when it was completed.

The project itself is unique and not a recurring activity

If a project repeats then it is actually a process that you can measure and improve each time you run it. Projects are more challenging because their unique nature means you have not seen the particular set of circumstances and problems before.

As an example, the design and development programme for the 'super-jumbo' Airbus A380 was a project. Designing the next model in the series will also be a new and unique project. However, manufacturing A380s is an impressive but nonetheless repetitive set of tasks that constitute a process – repeating each time that a plane is built from scratch.

A good project will have a couple of further attributes which, if missing, should immediately alert you to the fact that there is a problem.

There should be a well-defined objective for the project

Simple but vital if you are to convey to people what you are trying to achieve so they can understand:

- what the project will deliver;
- how the project needs to be integrated with other projects;
- how to prioritize the project against other options and resource uses.

There is a defined set of budget, resourcing and timescale constraints

A project that has the go-ahead should have a set of criteria defining a budget for resources (money, people, equipment, etc) and the overall completion time for the project.

WHAT IS PROJECT MANAGEMENT?

Project management has been compared to herding cats, keeping spinning plates on sticks and many other analogies that emphasize that it can be a very tricky and complex set of activities. A more formal description than 'project management' can be broken down into a number of elements.

Planning – what needs to be done.
This is where you regularly define the sequence, timing, resource requirements and dependencies of activities within the project.

Organizing – how it will be done. This means all aspects of selecting the project team, resources, facilities, communications, operations, meetings, etc.

Implementing – making it happen.
This is carrying out the planned activities.

Control – staying on course.
To keep the project on track you need to monitor progress relative to the plan. This includes:
- identifying and resolving issues;
- providing feedback on completion of milestones, progress of the overall project, future resource requirements, and risks.

All these aspects of managing projects will be explored in more detail in this book.

Within a project, there are only four factors that can ever be changed to achieve the desired result:

1. Specification (what is the project delivering?)
2. Quality (what is the quality of what is being delivered?)
3. Timescales (how long does it take you to get to any point?)
4. Resources (human, financial, technical, equipment, etc).

These four variables are inter-linked, and changing one will have an effect on the others. For example:

- reducing the timescales for a project requires an increase in resources if the specification and quality are to be maintained;
- if more resources are not available then reducing the specification may be necessary to complete a project in a given timescale without compromising quality.

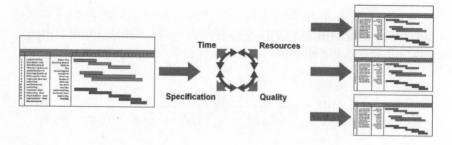

Figure 1.1 Producing different project scenarios

By altering one or more of these factors, the project manager can generate and consider different outcomes for the project.

These alternative 'what if' scenarios can be used by the project manager to find the most effective version of the plan. Different approaches and assumptions about these variables will provide different results to choose from. This won't always mean the quickest or the lowest cost. The most effective version can only be understood within the context of the situation surrounding the project. The scenarios can also provide evidence to senior management and/or customers about the impact of potential changes within the project.

WHY IS IT VITAL TO MANAGE PROJECTS WELL?

Good management of a project will provide you with critical information to help make decisions and keep the project on track. This information includes feedback on progress of the project against initial plans (where we are against where we expected to be), such as:

- estimated completion dates for key milestones;
- estimated overall completion date for the project;
- estimates of the ongoing resource requirements – what resources do we need now and what resources are assumed in the project in the future to achieve the current milestones and completion date?

It will also help in the management of risk and uncertainty: what are the risks identified in the project? What is their potential impact and what is being done to minimize or eliminate them?

PROJECT KILLERS

Doomed projects have a number of different, and sometimes subtle, characteristics that you need to understand if you are going to spot them in real life. The ability and attitude of the team can have an enormous impact on the project and so it is important to understand why teams sometimes can't, or won't, give you the true picture.

The Incompetent Team

The Incompetent Team won't even know they are in trouble. Although not malicious, the team members are just not experienced or switched on enough to realize that things are going wrong. They can't warn you the project is going badly but, even worse, they might tell you things are going well when they're not!

The Scared Team (Don't Shoot the Messenger)

The Scared Team members know they are in trouble but are not letting on!

Some project teams may have become wary of passing on 'the truth' as it is not dealt with in a positive way. Sticking their head above the parapet and telling their company's management or customers about problems only to be met with hostility and a 'shoot the messenger' mentality is either a real problem, or the team members believe it is.

The simple and human solution chosen by some teams is to stop telling anyone that there are problems. I call this the 'Scared Team syndrome'. Things are going wrong but, consciously or sometimes subconsciously, no one is passing on the bad news because they fear (rightly or wrongly) that nothing will be done or that they will be punished in some way.

The Ignored Team

This is frequently seen in the company where a 'stretch' target has been imposed that is way beyond what is achievable and management won't really listen to feedback on the problem. Target completion dates are imposed with little or no concern for what the team members are saying about whether they are achievable.

When the team members say they are working too hard there is little sympathy – in fact, there is often complaint that the management team are working too hard as well. 'You think you're working hard – I was working all Sunday', etc. This approach by management doesn't address the issue; it is just an attempt to get the team to go away and keep working long hours in the often vain hope that this will get the project completed. It's ostrich management, avoiding consideration and resolution of the problems in favour of platitudes and slave-driving.

Remember, this book is about having the evidence to enter discussions on deadlines, objectives and resources so that you can show the impact of decisions (or lack of them) on a project. It's far easier to achieve what you want during a discussion with senior management if you can clearly and credibly explain the exact effect of a change as opposed to just saying that it will be tricky. The evidence becomes the ammunition to defend the team where necessary and convince others of your position. If you don't have this evidence then arbitrary whims can render the project impossible to achieve.

The Doomed Team

From the outside, the Doomed Team looks similar to a Scared Team. A Scared Team fails to pass on information through fear. A Doomed Team does the same because the team believes failure is inevitable. They have lost faith in the ability to complete the project on time even if, in reality, the project is perfectly achievable.

Let's consider an example. A team has been working a plan to build a 52-storey skyscraper frame in a year. That looks like one storey a week will achieve the target, but after a month they have only completed one storey. One or two team members may now consider it tricky to deliver the project on time. Two months later only four storeys are complete. A few more team members may believe the project is going to fail now. Little by little, members of the team will be losing faith in the ability to complete the project but not necessarily telling the project manager.

The enormous problem with Doomed Teams is that they often lose belief while the project is still recoverable. They stop doing those extra things that projects need to succeed. The last-minute problem on Friday remains on their desk unresolved as they go away on leave. There's no point in doing it now as the project is 'doomed' anyway! This incorrect belief rapidly becomes self-fulfilling.

I should stress, this is not to say Doomed Teams don't care. In my experience, the reason Doomed Teams give up, even though the project is recoverable, is that they expect nothing can or will be done to help. This is where a project manager is needed who can do more than simply change the mechanics of the project and who can re-establish belief within the project team.

The Relaxed Team

Relaxed Team members may not be completely committed to the success of a project for a number of reasons. For example, they may:

- be retiring or leaving soon anyway;
- feel safe within a large organization that the project failure will not impact them in any way;
- be so jaded by relentless project over-runs that they are immune to worrying about problems as 'they always happen';
- have great job security.

Death by content

There are many teams delivering reams of project information that are so detailed that it is impossible for senior managers to understand, let alone react, to the situation. These enormous status documents do no one any favours.

The project team need to identify and communicate progress and any issues needing resolution. Expecting someone to read, and inwardly digest, a 100-page summary and plan each week is unrealistic. These documents won't be read and it will make it harder for the team to get approval for any changes as senior management won't have a clue what is going on.

'Everything goes right' plans

'Everything goes right' plans are surprisingly common. These plans assume there will be no problems and everything will go as planned. They are often the result of trying to meet constraints on time or resources that have been imposed and simply do not make allowance for anything going wrong.

They're fine if everything does go right, but it never happens that way. Plans of this type have no basis in reality, no room for contingency and no chance of success.

These plans are also frequently exacerbated by a lack of risk management during the life of the project. If a team doesn't recognize that things might go wrong they are unlikely to identify and manage risks properly as the project proceeds.

2

Dead Project Walking – Why some projects must be killed

Companies can be outstanding at generating new ideas – I mean really world-class – and yet they struggle to exploit them. One explanation is that the companies frequently don't have the resources they need. I'm not talking about the resources not existing in the company, I am talking about them being tied up doing other things.

If the resources are being used for something that is more valuable to the business than a project being delayed then that is probably a good use of the resources. If not, then the resource prioritization across the portfolio of projects isn't working.

However, at least this is a conscious decision – even if it's incorrect. The more frustrating problem for companies is when their resources are 'lost' to the business by working on bad projects or doing 'after sales' work on projects that have already been finished.

Colleagues of mine visited an R&D site and found that a staggering 90 per cent of time spent was actually trying to fix things in projects that had already been signed off as completed.

Management were completely unaware of this as their resource management system could not attribute individuals to tasks, so they could not track who was doing what.

WHY DEAD PROJECTS LIVE ON

These problems exist if the business does not understand what people are doing. I know that seems ridiculous but I've seen it enough to realize that resource management can be truly appalling without visibly crippling an organization – the company just runs as if through treacle and delivers far less than it could.

The Scared Project Manager

Before this chapter becomes a witch hunt against project team members, let me introduce you to the Scared Project Manager.

It may be that the project manager has become personally identified with a particular project or perhaps the project has a very high profile in the company. For whatever reason, the pressure on the project manager to succeed has increased and he or she is now too scared to pass on any bad news. He or she may be like a 'rabbit in the headlights' and be paralysed until the project crashes or they just have to leave the company.

The Vegas Project Manager

There's a phrase in poker called going 'on tilt'. It is used when someone loses control of his or her emotions and starts betting wildly. Well, I've seen a few project managers that you would have to say were the same.

As the project proceeds, they become aware that things are going badly but they remain optimistic that things can be turned around, and keep betting they'll succeed.

This means that sometimes they will be sinking money into a project that is doomed and should be killed off. However, they have lost perspective and don't want to give up when they should. They may feel their reputation is on the line or their ego might be in the driving seat, but you must assess projects rationally and sometimes you have to kill them.

Sunk costs

A principle in accounting is that you ignore 'sunk costs'. These are the costs that have already been committed to a given point.

It doesn't matter if you've already spent £1 or £50 million on a project to a given point. If the money that remains to be spent is greater than the benefits for the company, the project should be halted.

Did you read that right? Yes: even if you have committed £50 million to date then the rational decision in this case is to stop the project. Whether the company can make a rational decision and stop the project is another matter.

Political implications

Imagine there is only one project that is keeping a division of a company busy, eg the only boat being built in a shipyard. Even when the project goes severely over budget, it may be politically impossible to stop it as it would involve serious lay-offs or redundancies.

Alternatively, if the CEO has announced a major project to the stock market, the damage to the ego of the Chief Executive and/or the stock price of the company may mean cancelling the project is not an option.

There's no way to kill projects!

A genuine problem that keeps resources tied up doing the wrong things is the lack of a mechanism to actually 'kill' projects. Surprised? Again, there are companies that start projects and assume that if something was started it must be a good idea and therefore should be completed. Think about it: the company may start several projects in a given area and successful completion of the first project may render the other projects completely superfluous because:

- the problem has been resolved or gone away;
- the technical performance target has been achieved;
- the solution created by the successful project is not compatible with the other projects.

What I'm saying is that if you don't actually have an ongoing review process that can kill or put projects on hold, then you will have far fewer resources at your disposal and therefore you will start far fewer new projects.

Companies need a project review process that can also kill, or put on hold, projects for performance reasons if they:

- cannot meet a milestone (a milestone being a project-specific state of achievement, as will be discussed later);
- fail a gate review (a predefined step in a process that some companies use and through which new ideas/concepts, etc have to pass); and the important addition is...
- the project no longer makes sense with respect to other projects that have been completed or are in progress and other projects that are awaiting approval.

Part II

Where Are We?

Just because there is a plan does not mean the project is under control. Just because someone says the project is under control doesn't mean they are right.

When you are first given an existing project to take over, you will probably be handed a thick pile of project plans, status reports, etc. You have two options at this point. You can believe everything you are told or you can find out for yourself. If you believe everything you are told then you are going to find the world of project management full of surprises – few of them enjoyable.

The objective of Chapter 3 is to explain how to assess the status of an ongoing project. If you have been put in charge of the project, or are just trying to assess it, the chapter will not prove that the project is going well, but it will show if it is going particularly badly.

3

Diagnosing an Existing Project

WHY DOING A DIAGNOSTIC MAKES SENSE

When you are given a project to take over, you have a short period when you can discover and report any serious issues or problems. However, you need to know as soon as possible whether you have been handed a disaster in the making. Wait too long and when things start to go wrong they will be blamed on you!

There are two important factors that you will need to understand to identify if there are major problems with the project. First, you need to know if the team is competent enough in running a project to know where they really are. Second, if the team knows what they are doing then do they actually believe the project is on track? Chapter 1 describes some of the reasons why even a competent team is sometimes unwilling to communicate the real status of a project.

GETTING TO THE TRUTH

It is important for a project manager to motivate the team to work with him or her. I know that seems a strange concept. The team's being paid so they should be professional, right? However, if team members have experienced difficult projects with ineffective management and arbitrarily imposed dates, had problems ignored, inaccurate plans, etc, then they will need some convincing that this project is going to be different with you as project manager. I repeat: it is vital the team is motivated to work with the project manager.

I go into more detail about how you manage the team in Chapter 4, but here is how you start a diagnostic – you need to talk to the person who was in charge of the project before you.

Talking to the previous project manager

The first person to speak to, if possible, is the previous project manager. He or she can be an invaluable source of advice and tips about dealing with the project team, senior management, customers, etc. In essence, he or she can tell you where the icebergs are.

If your predecessor describes a series of problems with the project then you already have a partial answer to your question. The project may be in trouble and you need to make sure this is clear for senior management either as you take it over or as you decide not to take it on (if that luxury is open to you). Do bear in mind though that the previous project manager may actually have been incompetent and is trying to justify being replaced by exaggerating any problems.

If the previous project manager says everything is fine and on track, that may be good news but you can't simply assume this is correct – you need to keep digging.

Talking to the project team

Next it's time to talk to members of the project team. Remember that this can only confirm there are problems with the project at this point – you cannot prove it is going well!

In my experience, assessing the project works best when done informally. Getting team members in a room and hoping they will voice their deepest, darkest concerns to someone they have only just met is unrealistic. Go around the project team and try to have a word with individuals when they are alone. It's a good time to introduce yourself and you can get to the questions shown in Figure 3.1.

If you get a 'No' at any point then you need to investigate further because this is a sign of a potentially serious problem. Let's look at these questions in more detail.

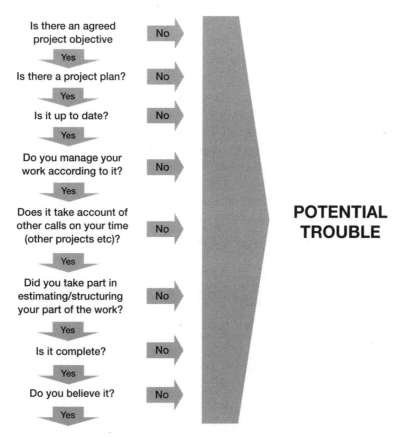

Figure 3.1 Talking to the project team

Is there an agreed project objective?

You're looking for evidence that the team are working to a clear statement of the objectives of the project. If this is entirely missing then I'm not sure how the project can ever succeed.

If only a few team members understand the objectives then you need to consider how the project is being run. However, it is not a problem for some team members to be unaware of the objectives if the project is being managed in line with them. It's not how I prefer to do things but if they are being managed so they operate 'as if' they knew the objectives then that is acceptable.

If someone isn't familiar with the objectives for the project then ask them:

- What are the targets for the project?
- What targets are they working to personally?
- How is the work they do specified?

You will find some team members are directed completely by others, so they do not understand the 'big picture', but what they do is in line with achieving success for the project. That is not a reason to press the panic button at this point but you need to work out where the direction is coming from and ensure it's consistent with the objectives.

If there is no evidence of an objective (no paper description or evidence of the team following one) then you know there is definitely a problem.

Is there a project plan?

If no one has sight of a project plan then the project will be in trouble. Without one, the team can't review against progress, identify problems early and resolve them before they become crises. It's like trying to get somewhere without a map. You have no idea where you are in relation to your destination so don't know if you're late, if you need to speed up, etc.

Is the project plan complete?

If the project plan is not complete then again there is a problem. This does not mean that you have to plan everything in intricate detail three years in advance – that would indicate a different problem. However, there should not be any segments of work or major tasks that are not on the project plan that are due in the near future. If there are gaps the plan is unlikely to reflect the true picture of the project.

If you find gaps then make sure you try to understand why and get some idea of their likely impact.

Do you manage your work according to the plan?

There may be a complete plan, but if team members are essentially ignoring it then that part of the plan does not represent reality. The difference between what the plan says should be done and what is actually done may be minor or very serious, but a plan that does not reflect what people are doing should be treated with suspicion.

Does it take account of other calls on your time?

The plan may be complete and people may be deciding which tasks they are doing on the basis of the plan, but does it reflect their real availability? There are many small jobs we need to do that would take five minutes to complete but are left for months because there are other calls on our time.

Tasks within projects are just the same. There may be a task clearly assigned to someone, but that does not mean he or she will do it when you expect. If you don't know what else that person is doing then you have no means of knowing when the task will be done. You can't run a big project with everyone telling you when they'll do every task because sometimes they'll be wrong, and you'll be relying on their ability to estimate how long their current workload will take and so will be at the mercy of the massive variation in people's ability to estimate. You'll have ultra-conservative estimates alongside hopelessly optimistic ones.

You're the project manager – you need to take control of estimation so that you can be satisfied with the information in the plan. It's your butt on the line!

To be accurate, the plan needs to take account of other activities that team members are undertaking, such as:

- other projects;
- management;
- meetings;
- holidays;
- training.

Ask the team members if the project manager knows about all the other demands on their time. If this is not the case, the duration of the team members' work shown in the plan will be wrong. (This will be explored further later in the book.)

Do you believe the plan?

This is a kind of catch-all question that is worth asking. Things may appear fine but this question may yield something interesting – a previously unspoken concern, issues within the team, or something they did not feel comfortable mentioning earlier in the conversation.

If you get this far without any issues then the project is not obviously broken, but just occasionally I have uncovered a major problem at this point.

DIGGING INTO THE PLAN

If you've had acceptable answers from the team, you can start looking at the plan.

It is far easier to investigate the electronic version of a project plan than a print-out. If you aren't familiar with the software being used then borrow someone who is up to speed with it to help you dig into the plan.

Are the key dates achievable and consistent?

You should look at dates both for milestones and for the end of the project. Consider whether these dates appear realistic and whether they meet internal/external constraints and requirements for the project, such as:

- contractual obligations;
- dates for handovers to other departments (eg development to manufacturing);
- market windows (eg getting a product in time for a particular event – Christmas, the Olympics, etc).

Are external inputs into the plan on course?

If there are key elements within the plan that are delivered from other projects or from outside the organization, are these on target?

Talk to the relevant project manager to get initial feedback on whether his or her part of the project will be delivered on time.

Does the high-level structure of the plan appear logical?

In project terms, an example of a logical problem might be a plan that has the roof being put on before the walls are erected.

Check through and see if there is anything obvious that jumps out at you as being strange. Ask more questions to clarify any concerns you have. You certainly won't be able to spot every error in project logic but you'll catch some and also signal to the project team that you are keeping an eye on everything.

Is the resourcing realistic?

By talking to the team you have already identified if the time allotted to work on the project is realistic. I'll illustrate this resource problem with an example.

I went into a development programme once and looked at the project plan. It looked good. That's the problem with Microsoft Project (and PowerPoint) – the biggest, steaming pile of junk can be made to look good. What makes this worse is that few senior managers have the experience to spot a poor project plan when they're two inches away from it.

I started by checking the resource usage in the plan. The very first person I checked was down to do 56 hours work on the following Monday. It became clear that this level of unreality was repeated throughout the plan. No one bothered checking and the project manager was both new to the company and completely inexperienced. When the real availability for the team was used, the overall duration lengthened by 700 per cent before any optimization.

The final version of the plan ended up 250 per cent longer than the team thought when I arrived. As I've shown, the earlier questions for the team can help prove a project is in trouble within a day (although they can't prove the project is going well). However, they were unnecessary in this case. One question identified one severely broken project.

Assuming someone can put in a full eight-hour day of moving project tasks forward is unrealistic enough; letting the plan suggest they'll do 56 is insane. The result is that the end date for a project mis-planned in this way will be wildly optimistic – even though the plan apparently looks sensible. People will not be able to get through the work as fast as the plan suggests and it will be significantly late.

You need to look at the resource usage to see if individuals or groups are over-allocated with work. The usage can be displayed graphically by project management software, as shown in Figure 3.2.

The bars above the 100 per cent usage line show that the resource 'RJ' has more work to do on every day of the project than there is time available. There will normally be a number associated with this over-allocation. In Figure 3.2 the highest bar is actually a 500 per cent over-allocation of work for this resource. In other words you would need six resources like this to carry out the work planned on some of these days.

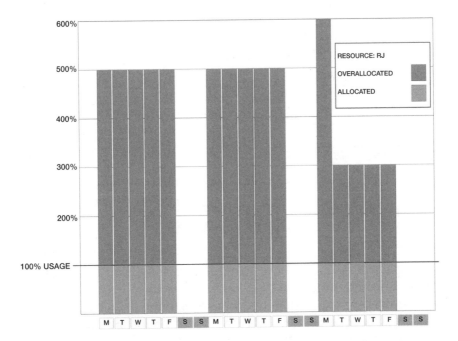

RESOURCE: RJ

OVERALLOCATED

ALLOCATED

Figure 3.2 Resource usage chart

An individual should never be allocated more than 100 per cent for any day. However, groups of resources are different. Imagine that you have six installation engineers in the plan. They can reasonably be used to show up to 600 per cent effort in a day (100 per cent each). The maximum number of resources in a group should be defined in the plan and so the software will also show where groups are over-allocated with work. If you only have six field engineers then a figure of 700 per cent effort on one day would be an over-allocation.

If you spot significant over-allocation of resources in a plan, it is a sign that the previous project manager or planner was not really up to speed and you will need to revisit the plan in detail. The only thing you know with certainty is that the duration of the project is going to increase as a result of any corrections.

Are there any unrealistic constraints on dates?

Start and end dates for tasks can be constrained in a variety of ways. For example, you can set a task so that it 'must start on' or 'cannot start before' a given date. This can be very useful but it is best to limit the use of these constraints as using too many can swiftly lead to all sorts of headaches, with tasks set to start before the preceding tasks have finished.

Look through the plan for any constrained dates and check the logic behind the constraint. If there is no logical reason for the constraint then remove it and prepare for the plan to look considerably worse afterwards in terms of duration.

DIAGNOSING A MULTI-COMPANY PROGRAMME

If the project extends across several companies, you may need to repeat this diagnosis in each company. You may not be responsible for the actual management of other parts of the project but, if there are dependencies between the different parts of the projects (and there are bound to be), then the other companies have the capacity to sink the project.

What you do will depend on what is possible and also on your company's status in the overall project. If:

- **you are just delivering a component into a larger system**, you may only need to worry about your part of the programme;
- **your project is dependent on input from other projects** in the programme, you ideally need to assess if these are going to happen when you expect;
- **you are managing the whole programme**, you need to assess the state of project management in the other companies. The approach described above will work perfectly well to get some feel for whether any reported progress is likely to be accurate.

The difference when you talk to people in another company is that they are likely to be wearing a company hat and will be less open to telling you the truth about the situation. This is a very human reaction but it means you have to dig carefully and minimize any concerns they may have about problems being caused by talking to you.

Make a decision

What you do next will depend on the situation.

If you are committed to the project, the next step is perhaps to warn senior management that there are some issues and that you are now going to get a handle on the exact situation.

If you have an option about whether or not you take on the project, it's down to you to decide how you proceed. Talking to the team should have given you a feeling for whether things appear fixable or whether they are critically out of control. Your next action will depend on how you feel about all the other variables surrounding the project – your exposure if it fails, the importance of the project, how rejecting the project will reflect on you, etc. Only you can decide. Taking on a failing project is high risk but can also be high reward in terms of your career.

If you're staying with the project, the next chapter will show you how to gain control – and keep it!

Part III

Getting the Right Initial Plan

If you are here, it is because you are either starting a new project (good luck) or you trying to get control of an existing one (even more luck required).

This section of the book will show you how to structure the project to create a realistic view with the current assumptions about timescales, resources, specifications and quality of delivery.

4

Leading Projects

To show what it takes to be a good project manager, it is useful to first consider the characteristics of bad ones.

THE WRONG KIND OF PROJECT MANAGERS

We've probably all seen at least one of these characters.

The Micro-manager

Some project managers may try to micro-manage the life out of a project but ultimately it is counterproductive. These project managers end up alienating their team by conveying the feeling that they have no confidence in them. If the team members feel every small decision is made by the project manager they won't take personal responsibility for anything.

In addition, project managers just cannot be involved in every detail of larger projects. It's impossible unless they have invented a time machine or found a way to clone themselves. By trying to monitor everything, they can't concentrate on deciding what needs to be managed and won't have the time to properly manage what is actually important.

The Panicker

This sort of person races around at full speed, swearing, shouting and generally looking worried. They don't pass on any confidence in the project team and tend to stress other people out. They seem to think that manic action in any direction is a good substitute for knowing where you are going.

Sometimes there is no substitute for raising your voice to get a point across or to underline that something is exceptionally serious. However, if you are shouting all the time you have no headroom left to escalate things to show your displeasure even more clearly – unless you want to try stamping up and down and screaming and screaming like a 6-year-old.

BEING THE RIGHT KIND OF PROJECT MANAGER

Many people have had experience of a badly run project. Far fewer have experienced a well-run and successful one.

Projects aren't won from your desk. Get to know your project team and, on larger projects, ensure you at least know all the team leaders and work package managers. This allows you to 'set the tone' for the project and people are more likely to discuss problems with you if they have met you.

As a project manager, you have the opportunity to run your project effectively and, at the same time, demonstrate to the others in the team how it's done. To do this you need to overcome the natural cynicism and fatigue of people who have probably heard and seen it all. They may well have done the detailed planning of this or other projects time and again, only to find the results ignored or left inside a filing cabinet to rot!

If you want your project to succeed you may have to convince these people that it will be different this time. This means you have to make them understand that you are different from most project managers they have worked with previously.

You need to work in a new way and also be totally consistent in doing what you say. Make sure you don't give the team the chance to think you are 'just like every other project manager'. Be consistent, educate the team, and show you are not only leading the team but also passing on project management skills that will be very valuable to them in the rest of their career.

Work like you're in the organization for life. Don't screw your boss – it never pays. Don't mistreat your team members – the time may come when you're working for one of them and they will not have forgotten how you worked with them.

You don't have to be Brad Pitt but…! In 1999, finding a project manager was tough. All the contract project managers were being snapped up to run Y2K projects and so you took what you could get and you paid dearly for it. The project I was working on came up with a gem of a contract project manager. He was a thoroughly nice and decent man but sadly one who inspired no sense of confidence at all.

The 'royal flush' event occurred when he managed to carry out in one meeting all of the bad habits that undermined him with the team. He arrived late for the morning meeting (strike one), asked if he could borrow a pad to write on (strike two), and then a loose, false tooth fell out as he spoke (strike three – you're out). Any one of these events would have been unfortunate, but all three together really destroyed any confidence anyone had in him.

GIVE THE TEAM RESPONSIBILITY

The single greatest thing you can do within a project is make it clear that the responsibility for delivery of a particular element rests with the people doing the work. You are there to help them, support their efforts, brainstorm new approaches, find other resources, motivate them or kick their butts when it's needed, but **they have responsibility for delivery**.

In my experience, giving people responsibility has a galvanizing effect on them. It shows you have faith in them but also makes them more determined to succeed as they now have ownership of this part of the project. It gives them the opportunity to shine.

This doesn't mean that you don't monitor what is going on, but it does mean you don't micro-manage the hell out of your team. You provide support where needed, monitor the project so you know where to apply your time and effort, and respond when you are asked for help.

MANAGING IN A MATRIX

In some projects you are working with a team that also reports to you as their line manager. They are very likely to do exactly as directed (unless they are really stupid) as you hold the key to their pay rises, working conditions, personnel reviews, etc.

In a matrix organization, you are likely to have a project team that is not necessarily made up of people who report to you directly – teams are formed around projects from across different resource groups; see Figure 4.1. You may be responsible for the project but you do not have positional power over people in the project team.

This means you are dealing with a group of people whose futures you cannot directly affect. They may or may not believe in the project, may or may not understand if the project is going well and, if it is going badly, may or may not have told anybody.

It is vital that the project is run as well as possible because these are not people you can hire and fire, these aren't people who are scared of you or beholden to you for their pay rises. These people are essentially independent and more concerned with their line management relationship. So how do you make this work?

It is important to understand the resourcing requirements for the project and get commitment from resource managers as early as possible, rather than recognizing the potential problems late in the day and trying to recover the situation at the last moment. The latter approach can backfire when you discover that the team members aren't committed to you – they are committed to keeping their jobs!

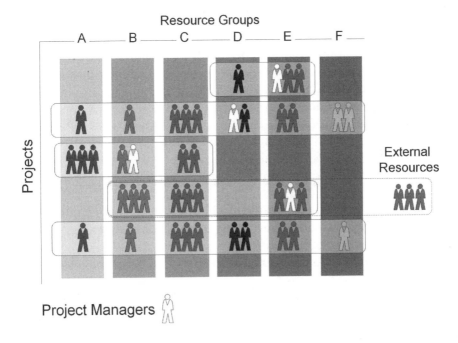

Figure 4.1 Project teams in a matrix organization

BEING A TEAM PLAYER

Keep your ego at bay. You want the team to be able to tell you bad news and also (politely) point out when you are wrong. If you wed yourself to your opinions and put down anyone daring to question you, you will have lots of surprises during the project – mainly unpleasant.

There are likely to be other projects within the company that rely on some of the resources being used in your project. This presents a couple of challenges to you as project manager.

First, as project manager, you can try to jealously guard resources assigned to your project to the detriment of every other project. Keeping them working solely on your project may appear to provide the best chance of success for your project. However, there will almost certainly come a point where you need to change your resources at short notice and, if you have a reputation for ruthlessly ring-fencing your resources, then it's less likely other project managers will be flexible and help you out. Another problem with ring-fencing your resources is that you may actually damage the company by your actions.

Imagine that some of your team members are working on a non-critical part of your project. There may be plenty of time in hand for that particular set of tasks and no doubt they can finish with time to spare. Those people might also be required on a time-critical part of a much larger or more important project. Keeping them to yourself makes no material difference to your project but may well cause the other project to fail. Would that be the right thing to do? Will people be congratulating you on the success of your project if they understand the knock-on effect?

Now reverse the situation and imagine you need the people for your project and the lower priority project they are already working on engaged is being run by someone else. That's the time when you do everything you can to get hold of those people. By having a realistic project plan you will have the evidence you need to show why they *must* come to your project.

My advice is simple: play nice whenever you can and play smart but hard when you can't.

Set the standard you expect of others. You cannot personally monitor everything in the project but you can consistently instil the standards you expect in your team. They can then do the monitoring on your behalf.

OVERCOMING 'IT CAN'T BE DONE'

When someone tells you, 'It can't be done', you have a number of choices. The only one I would not recommend is simply accepting their opinion, or 'giving up' as I like to call it. They may be right but it may also signal that they:

- don't have a clue how to resolve the problem (and have either given up or don't want to show their ignorance);

- can't be bothered to look for an answer;
- are too busy to have looked at the problem yet.

There are other explanations but your job as project manager is to get these people into the right frame of mind to start considering other options. The following approaches can be useful where you feel the issue can actually be resolved. Ideally you only want to go through these questions as far as is necessary to get the right answer for you.

Ask why it can't be done

This may show you why it really can't be done, or trigger the thinking of the person you are speaking to. (I have seen this result in people changing their opinion on the spot.)

Challenge the assumption

'If I gave you a million pounds to fix it would you be able to do it?' This consistently raises a smile and sometimes immediate agreement that it can be done provided the reward really is available.

There are some other similar questions you can use here too. How would our competition get around this? If we were able to solve this, how would we do it?

What else have we tried or could we try?

Sometimes going back to previous attempts can be very useful and again, rather than arguing whether it can be done or not, you are exploring means to do it.

If I gave you unlimited resources and budget would it still be impossible?

It's worth a try. You don't have unlimited anything but if they admit it's possible then you are simply discussing how a change in resourcing could still achieve the result.

Who else understands this problem as I'd like a discussion about this issue?

In reality you don't necessarily want the discussion but you do want to know who else can talk about this issue and also test the person's resolve that the problem cannot be fixed. When they know you will be speaking to someone else about it you can sometimes see them start to back-pedal.

Can you go away and think about it again?

Sometimes you want to put a bit of pressure on an individual or team. If you really don't think they are trying hard enough then ask them to go away and think about it again. If you're convinced there is a way through, give them a deadline and tell them to come back with at least one potential solution.

All these questions do is kick someone's thinking sideways slightly to make them consider how something can be done instead of justifying why it can't!

An officer responsible for nuclear submarine maintenance was summoned to a meeting by the base commander.

Replacing the diesel generator in one of the submarines was a very costly and long process that involved cutting a hole through the side of the submarine. The senior officer turned to him in front of the contractor due to carry out such a replacement and said, 'Thank you but we can replace the generator ourselves and it will be done in four months.'

At that point there was no way to carry out a generator replacement that quickly. The senior officer was bluffing the contractors and laying down a challenge to his team.

Knowing they had to achieve the impossible, the officer responsible went with several others and started to measure the space around the generator. They made diagrams, they designed special rigs to lift the generator and then trolleys to move the generator around. And they succeeded!

I'm not advocating asking the impossible of your team, but challenging their thinking can sometimes get extraordinary results!

FOCUSING YOUR ATTENTION
IN THE RIGHT PLACES

When you are talking to members of the team, you need to get to the core of the issues rather than scratching the surface. The challenge is that drilling down into the detail of every aspect of a project will be difficult unless you live on coffee and intend giving up sleeping for a while. Micro-managing everything is unpopular with teams and is a poor use of everyone's time.

The solution is to identify where you should invest your time and, just as important, where you shouldn't. Of course this can be easier said than done on occasion.

Clearly, it's obvious that further discussion is necessary if:

- someone tells you there is a problem in a part of the project;
- evidence of problems emerges (eg test failures, delays in delivery, conflict);
- you know the person is very inexperienced or needs close attention and help.

However, what if no one tells you anything is wrong? How do you tell where you should be managing and where you should be leaving the team to get on with things?

This is where I feel it is important to be in face-to-face contact with your team and team leaders. Where people have concerns that they are not expressing then you can spot several behaviours that indicate further investigation may be needed.

Avoidance

This can be seen in a number of different ways when people:

- continually veer the subject away from a particular topic;
- postpone meetings;
- delay delivery of information;
- continually provide excuses for why things aren't progressing as expected;
- are generally evasive.

When you see one of these behaviours then you need to check that the situation is OK. Sometimes this may be very quick: 'Everything OK?', 'Yeah, fine.'

Other times you'll 'look under a rock' and find a pile of something smelly and another rock. Look under that and you'll find a worse stench... and another rock!

Over-talking

This is when you ask a simple question and you get an enormously complex answer that you weren't expecting and that seems disproportional to the subject. When people talk significantly more than usual this can be a sign that they are nervous and so they keep adding and adding points to their reply in the hope that you'll be satisfied with the answer. If this happens you should dig deeper into the issue with them in a one-to-one discussion. You can try to discuss it in the middle of a meeting, but it will be easier to get to the truth without an audience, and you won't win any friends if you end up embarrassing one of the team members in public.

Using silence to get more information from people

Silence can be the most powerful tool in a discussion. If you ask someone a question and you aren't satisfied with the answer then you can, of course, ask for more information, get clarification of a particular detail or whatever. However, before you do that, you can also stay silent for a few moments.

People normally become very uncomfortable when there is a lull in a conversation and will try to fill an awkward silence by talking some more. This is particularly true when they are worried about something and don't want to talk about it – even if the discomfort is only subconscious.

I don't recommend following every question with a 30-second pause, as people will either think you're a pain in the backside or a moron. However, I do think the careful use of silence can be very powerful in the right place. When you do uncover serious issues in this way, you shouldn't feel all smug and triumphant. Victory dances are sadly out of order as you need to get on with fixing the problem. The motto should be, 'We are where we are', and you need to deal with the problem first.

Japanese factories became famous for having lights that indicated if part of the production process had a problem. If the light went on, people would come running. They weren't coming to start playing 'blame-finger' or to berate their colleagues – they were there to fix things fast!

It may be that you have to investigate and then address the causes of a particular problem, but try to concentrate on solving the problem first and then fixing what caused the problem later on.

5

Project Scope and Initiation

INTRODUCTION

Efficiency is doing things right; effectiveness is doing the right things. (Drucker)

Organizations only have limited resources at their disposal and one of the greatest management challenges is using those resources in the best way possible. This means choosing between alternatives, and project managers need to play their part by providing the right level of information to allow decisions to be made.

Launching a new project ties up human, financial and technical resources and so approval can only happen when there is enough information to make an intelligent choice.

'Keep it simple, stupid!' is a commonly used phrase for very good reason. Don't over-engineer, over-complicate or generally over-do anything in the project.

You probably can't afford the extra design time, cost of fabrication, time to debug, etc. This doesn't mean you should under-engineer things – just get the right balance.

When a project is considered for approval, there are many reasons why it may not be accepted. For example:

- resources necessary for the project are not available;
- the returns are lower than for a similar project concept;
- there are no market channels to exploit the project deliverables;
- the technology risk is too high;
- the project is considered too expensive;
- the project concept is too similar to an existing project;
- the concept falls outside the current business strategy;
- the project concept does not meet 'customer' needs.

To bring together the information to decide if a project should be launched, there needs to be some form of structured project kick-off that will detail the scope and objectives of the proposed project. This is known as 'project initiation'.

PROJECT INITIATION

To initiate a project, organizations need to appoint a project manager *before* the project is approved. This means the project manager will sometimes take a project concept through to approval – only for it to be rejected. However, the project manager role is vital at this point in the life of the project – ensuring all the different parties are consulted and drawing together the information needed to make the right decision.

One major transport provider is constantly refitting its infrastructure but it does not include project managers during the project scoping work. Projects are approved by a team dedicated to launching projects and the project manager is only appointed after approval!

This creates problems because members of the scoping team have no experience of managing one of these projects and so do not understand the reality of infrastructure builds and refits. As a result, their budget estimates and schedules are frequently miles away from the real cost of the projects and their methodologies are not always the fastest way to get the work done.

The obvious recommendation is that they appoint project managers to take part in the scoping process. This means the person most liable for the success or failure of the project will have a chance to influence it before it is approved. In addition, the project managers should be broadening the experience of their scoping team so that they can help spread new and effective practices across the organization.

Forming the definition team

Once appointed, the project manager needs to assemble a team around him or her that is capable of carrying out the definition phase.

Keep the core project team as small as possible whilst including the skills you need and delivering the project. Having more people than is necessary increases the communication overhead and opportunities for mistakes.

This team defining the project is unlikely to be identical to the team that actually executes it, but must nonetheless have the relevant skills, experience and knowledge necessary.

By the time a project has gone through the approval process, some of the scoping team may not be free or more suitable resources may have become available.

Surround yourself with good people. It's as true in a project as it is in a business. The team members are the ones who will deliver the project, so try to get the best people you can.

Objectives

The objectives of project initiation are to:

- ensure that the project is understood and approved by relevant parties;
- understand the feasibility and level of risk;
- identify an internal champion (sponsor);
- identify a 'customer' for the project – someone who actually wants the project to be carried out. If you haven't got a 'customer' then you shouldn't have a project;
- commit the resources necessary for the initial phases;
- understand the overall resource requirements (human, financial, technical);
- understand how the project fits into the existing portfolio;
- evaluate whether the project should proceed;
- ensure that the project manager has agreement and backing for the project.

If you inherit a project and you can't identify who is the sponsor (or the 'customer') then things are seriously in trouble. Don't mess around with too much diagnosis: just go back to the person who has appointed you to try to understand why the project is going ahead. If you still can't figure out a good reason why the project exists, then it probably shouldn't. Don't be afraid to kill projects. Remember organizations would be a lot better off if they could identify and kill doomed or pointless projects early.

It is important to have a senior manager who is championing the project and willing to go to bat for you when you hit problems (and you will). Think of this champion as the proverbial 500-pound gorilla who is going to bash through obstacles in your path and help you drive the project to a successful completion. Make sure you keep the champion informed and keep him or her on side with the project – even if things are going badly.

Surprising bad news hurts far worse than bad news you've been warned about beforehand. This doesn't mean you need to confess every error, concern or problem, but you should keep the sponsor informed of realistic progress in the project and warn where help may be needed in advance.

The outcome of project initiation is a document that describes the scope of the project in terms of objectives, resourcing, risks, work breakdown, etc. It is called the 'Project Charter'.

THE PROJECT CHARTER

 The Project Charter is a structured document that describes the key aspects of the plan including objectives, work plan, resourcing, risks and budget.

At the end of the project initiation work there will be a point where the Project Charter will be reviewed and a decision taken on whether the project should be cleared to proceed, be put on hold, or rejected by the organization.

If the project is accepted, it immediately enters the more detailed planning and execution phase. The Project Charter then becomes the reference point for the project in terms of deliverables, timescales, etc.

Specifications are like water – sometimes they creep like a glacier, sometimes they sweep past you like an avalanche.

A strong and clear Project Charter agreed by all parties provides the ammunition you need to resist most of the 'specification creep' you will encounter.

CREATING THE PROJECT CHARTER

The work required, and level of detail, will vary enormously depending on the size of the project. For example, digging the Channel Tunnel is clearly orders of magnitude more complex and inherently risky than writing a business database. The level of information needed to formally launch the project is therefore very different.

To create the Charter the project manager should:

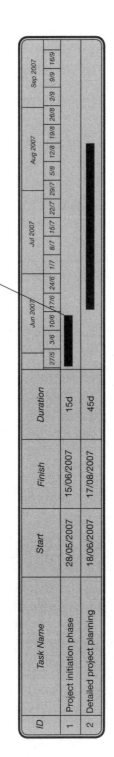

Figure 5.1 Project initiation

- Ensure that team members who will actually deliver the project are closely involved in developing it wherever possible.
- Obtain input and approval from internal stakeholders, 'customers' (whether internal or external) and the project champion/sponsor.
- Carefully control changes to the Charter once the project is launched.

The best way to start this process is with a kick-off meeting. This will help create some of the content of the Charter and also allow you to plan how you will work with the team to deliver the completed document.

If you have inherited an existing project then you need to go back and review the Charter carefully. It is safer to assume that the Project Charter on a troubled project is flawed until proven otherwise.

Whether you are creating the Project Charter from scratch or reworking an existing one, the Charter document should contain the sections and contents shown in Table 5.1.

The Project Charter is an excellent way of signalling the true impact of a project and getting early recognition and approval of some of the facts from senior managers and customers alike.

Now, let's be sensible for a second. That's a long list of contents and for some projects it will be overkill. Some projects will only need a couple of pages; others require hundreds. The key is to consider each section and put an appropriate level of detail into the document.

If you're the project manager, you need to ensure the Charter delivers the information necessary for all parties and no more. Enough is enough – once you've got sufficient detail to inform all the different parties, allow them to approve the project, then stop. Any more work on the Charter is a waste of time until the project is approved.

GET IT RIGHT EARLY ON – IT'S CHEAPER

The generic risks in a project reduce over time – the more work you do the less likely it is that there is a huge red flag lurking somewhere in the project. Let's consider a typical product development process to illustrate this.

Table 5.1 Project Charter contents

Section	Typical contents
Background/History	This section is a summary of the situation that has triggered the project. This might be a problem that has to be resolved or an opportunity that could be exploited by the company. Provide an overview of attempts that have been made to date to solve the problem/exploit the situation. Describe the impact on the business of not solving the problem/exploiting the situation. Include highlights from any business case developed to support the project.
Objectives	Include the objectives for the project.
Milestones	List the major milestones through to project completion as clear 'states of achievement'. If there are any clear decision points where the project logically could be halted, then these should also be described along with the criteria that would influence the decision, such as results in another project, revised time to completion against deadlines, etc.
Work breakdown	Show the breakdown of major and key work elements below the milestones. Describe key resource decisions already made or in question (eg using external resources for sensitive work packages).
Timescales	Outline the estimated timescales for completion of key milestones and the overall project – assuming the planned resourcing, specification and quality.

Table 5.1 Project Charter contents (*continued*)

Section	Typical contents
Risks and mitigation	Describe major risks to the project and the contingency or mitigation planned to minimize their probability of occurrence or impact.
Budget	Provide an estimate of the budget through to completion. Identify any cost areas that are currently speculative or susceptible to severe change.
Project organization	Identify the project manager, project team, customers (whether internal or external) and the senior team sponsor.
Tolerances	Tolerances within which the project manager can operate without escalating problems (eg the budget for a given phase).

Figure 5.2 shows the relative cost of having to change a design. This may not be mathematically identical for all projects but the principle is rock solid.

As you go through the process, the team has progressively more and more information to show that the product is satisfactory.

Developing the concept will weed out some problems and the feasibility study will eliminate some more. Each phase improves the level of understanding of the project and hence reduces the risk of delivering a 'bad' product/service/result. One second before the end of the project the risk is negligible as the team will have encountered, and must have resolved, all the problems to get to that point.

Conversely, the cost of eliminating an error increases the further you go through the process, as illustrated in Figure 5.3.

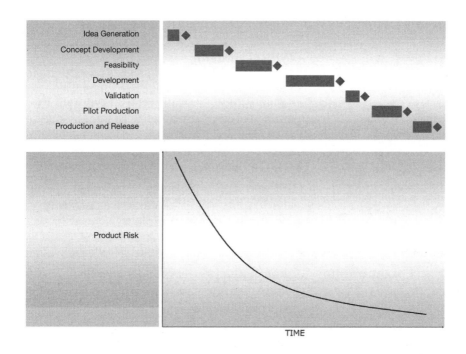

Figure 5.2 Risk reduces over the life of a project

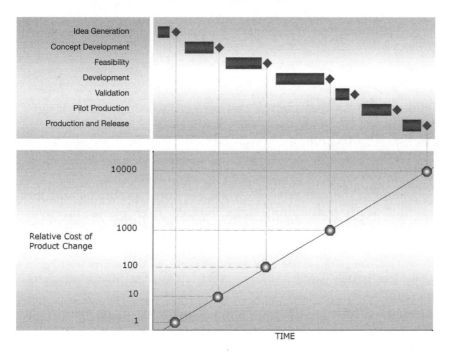

Figure 5.3 The costs to fix problems increase over the life of a project

As an example, consider the development of the McLaren F1. This car hit 240 mph (with a few minor modifications) with the programme costing £8.5 million to get the first car out of the door – including building the factory in which it was made.

In comparison, the Bugatti Veyron can travel 10 mph faster. The other difference is that the Veyron cost around £250 million to develop – which is expensive if you only sell 300 cars. The problem with the Veyron is that the boss, Ferdinand Piech, then head of the VW group, set up a BFHG (Big Fat Hairy Goal) of 250 mph (OK, it was 400 km/h to be precise) and 1,000 brake horsepower. Unfortunately this goal came with a big fat hairy price tag.

Gordon Murray and McLaren approached their project with a simpler goal – to build the best sports car ever. Simple, but clearly challenging to achieve. Bugatti, under the VW umbrella, set a massively challenging target without doing enough work to establish how feasible it was. Their sleek concept design was shown to the public early and hence could not be radically changed. It was subsequently found to have major problems with overheating due to the absence of vents. The same design led to serious stability problems, culminating in spinning the car at an early public appearance. They don't appear to have invested enough time or money early on in the concept and design phase – leading to massive problems later on in their development, nearly six years of delay and a massive overspend to put things right.

You have to believe the McLaren was designed hard then corrected lightly, with the reverse case for the Veyron. When the McLaren was built there was only one physical clash of a component against another that was not eradicated during design. The Veyron had 600 such clashes.

When companies have a big objective they need to invest early in planning and studies. Correcting a mistake on paper is several orders of magnitude less expensive than a correction during development, and is likewise far cheaper than a product recall or failure. It really is cheaper in the long run to get things right early.

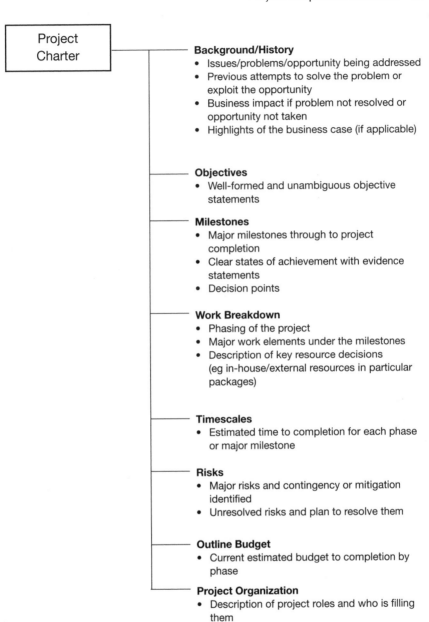

Figure 5.4 Contents of a Project Charter

Scope and initiation: summary and actions

1. The objective of project initiation is to ensure that a project is understood and approved by the relevant parties.
2. The Project Charter is a structured document that describes the key aspects of the plan including objectives, work plan, resourcing, risks and budget.

    Use members of the team who will actually do the work to help develop the information for the Charter.
3. To prepare the Project Charter for approval you will need to go through most of the elements described in the following chapters in this book.
4. Create the Project Charter only to the level of detail demanded by the particular project. Do enough work to generate the information needed by all parties in considering the project for approval, and no more.
5. The Project Charter should contain most of the elements shown in Figure 5.4.

6

Agreeing Objectives

If you have no clue where you are going – you will probably get there.

WHY OBJECTIVES ARE IMPORTANT

One of my colleagues was booking flights for a group meeting in Oslo. He informed me that I should buy the return flight myself and so I did.

When we got to the check-in for the outbound flight, the check-in lady looked a bit puzzled. After a moment she asked if we had booked together. It turned out that my colleague Stefan meant that I should book the return flight (as in both ways) whereas I took him at his word assuming he meant just the return leg. It's lucky we get on so well or it might have been a real 'fight or flight' moment.

We still laugh about it now and are insistent our own interpretation was correct – but obviously I'm right!

That is a simple misunderstanding of the type that happens every day. It was quickly recovered in this case, but misunderstandings in projects are often the cause of major problems or even disaster.

Feet or metres?

It doesn't make much difference when you use one measure of distance to someone used to working in the other. They might convert it in their head or ask you to use the other unit. Either way it's not a big issue.

However, when you are measuring the distance that a space probe should orbit above the surface of Mars then you absolutely need to agree on one or the other. Sadly the Mars Orbiter team didn't agree this between two different parts of the team.

The splattered remains may be found on the surface of the planet in the future, but the egg on the face of the engineering teams is visible to the naked eye.

This is why clear and unambiguous objectives are critical where work is defined between individuals, groups, companies, etc. If you don't get clarity then you are unlikely to have success.

Stating the objectives for a project allows all parties to contribute and agree the deliverables at the outset. A clearly defined set of objectives will ensure that everyone involved in managing, overseeing and delivering the project has a consistent document that achieves the following:

- defines agreed milestones and an end point for the project;
- ensures everyone understands what will be delivered;
- is understandable by all;
- supports correct delivery across boundaries between teams;
- lets you know when part of the project is complete.

Most projects have some statement of objectives. The problem is that they are frequently very poorly defined and allow room for confusion and misunderstandings.

Creating the set of objectives with all the parties involved in the project is therefore one of the most critical steps for the project manager. Trust me, time spent here will help you identify (and hopefully resolve) disagreements and misunderstandings between the various parties at the outset of the project. Finding out that the project's 'customer' has made a mistake about what they really need may give you someone to blame but leaves the project in bad shape and, by association, will reflect poorly on the project manager.

> The conditions you attach to commitments you make are always forgotten, but the commitment never is!

As project manager you have the potential to get at least some of the glory for a well-executed project (others will step in front of you when praise is being handed out), but you are also first in the firing line if it goes wrong. At that point you will notice the absence of people anywhere near you – let alone in front of you!

DEVELOPING WELL-DEFINED OBJECTIVES

> Running a project without clear objectives is like driving your car to a meeting blindfold. You might get there by luck but it will be painful and there will be casualties.

There are a number of ways of developing project objectives to try to ensure they are as complete as necessary.

SMART objectives

The most widely known approach to setting objectives is based on the acronym SMART. However, there doesn't appear to be complete agreement over what some of the letters mean so I'll explain both versions where there are differences.

SMART can be broken down into the following characteristics of a well-defined objectives statement.

Specific

Do the project's objectives make it clear what the exact targets are for the project?

Measurable

Is there an unambiguous way that you can 'measure' when the project's objectives have been met? In other words, can you look at the stated objectives and say the project is complete, knowing that no one can or will disagree with you?

Attainable/Achievable

Is it actually possible to achieve the objectives? If it really is impossible then you need to go back to the start and think again.

Realistic/Relevant

The 'attainable' criterion was about whether the objectives are possible. The 'realistic' term is often used to consider whether the project team is capable of achieving the objective. It may well be possible in theory but impossible for you in practice.

Running 100 metres in 9.75 seconds is 'attainable' in principle but sadly I'm never going to be able to run that fast without the aid of genetic manipulation, an enormous quantity of performance-enhancing drugs and a small rocket attached to me. It's attainable but just not realistic for me, sadly. The same thinking needs to be applied to your project.

The 'relevant' meaning of the R in SMART is also useful to make you consider whether the objective is an appropriate one for the project. Does it highlight all of the most important aspects of the project?

Timed

When will the project be completed? People need to know as it may well be linked to other projects for marketing, sales, distribution or whatever comes after your part is finished. You should get agreement on when you are aiming to finish before the project begins.

You'll notice that this is really a checklist for assessing a set of objectives once they're written to see what you've missed. You can't easily use SMART as a list of contents for an objectives document. However, the next approach can easily be used as a guide.

What, why, when, how, where and who

> I keep six honest serving-men
> (They taught me all I knew);
> Their names are **What** and **Why** and **When**
> And **How** and **Where** and **Who**. (Rudyard Kipling)

Kipling may not have been a project manager but he had the right idea. Those six words are a complete way to consider an objectives statement, as shown in Table 6.1.

Limit the use of acronyms in the project. Constantly using acronyms provides a barrier to understanding for newcomers and non-experts involved in the project, eg customers!

As an example, I can't tell if PC means personal computer, politically correct, programmable controller or police constable. One project I worked on had 720 TLAs (three-letter acronyms) and 80 FLAs (four-letter acronyms). That puts the learning curve somewhere between steep and vertical. Remember that you are striving for clarity among everyone involved in the project, so ditch the acronyms.

GOOD AND BAD OBJECTIVES – SOME EXAMPLES

Let's consider two very different objectives from history: two famous occasions with very different outcomes.

Table 6.1 What, why, when, how, where and who

Where are we and **why** are we doing this project?	You need to describe the context for the project so people understand the background – client needs, competitive situation, performance requirements, etc.
What are we going to do?	What is the project aiming to deliver?
How will we do it and **who** will do it?	Describe how you are going to deliver the project. What parts of the company will be working on it? Will there be other companies involved? What methods and techniques will be used?
How will we know when it's done?	What are the criteria for when the project is finished? The end point should define any testing or acceptance trials that the project must pass before it is complete.
What will we do next?	How does the project fit into other activities/projects? The next steps could be: • commercialization; • further phases; • transitions from research to development; • pilot trial to launch.

The Charge of the Light Brigade

The following order was given by Lord Raglan to a group of horse cavalry during the Battle of Balaclava in the Crimean War:

Lord Raglan wishes the cavalry to advance rapidly to the front, follow the enemy, and try to prevent the enemy carrying away the guns. Horse artillery may accompany. French cavalry is on your left. Immediate.

The cavalry followed the order (as they understood it) and rode into a valley defended by 20 battalions and 50 cannons. Caught with guns to the front, left and right of them, the cavalry had terrible casualties inflicted on them by an opposing cavalry force outnumbering them ten to one and infantrymen to all sides. This disastrous charge was immortalized in a poem by Lord Tennyson.

So where was the problem? In simple terms, the objective was not specific enough. The critical phrase was: 'Lord Raglan wishes the cavalry to advance rapidly to the front.' The cavalry did as they understood they were being told but didn't attack the correct 'front'.

Raglan wanted an emplacement attacked on the other side of the hill to the left-hand side of the valley. Instead he got his cavalry running the gauntlet right down the middle of the valley – surrounded on three sides and brutally cut down.

The order was not a well-defined objective as it was clearly not 'specific' or unambiguous ('where'). The good news is it was 'timed'. The doomed soldiers knew the order was to be carried out immediately.

Hopefully your projects won't run this badly, but the following is often true...

If anything is ambiguous then the meaning chosen will be the worst possible for the project.

Let's now look at a very different objective that was good enough to help galvanize a nation behind an extraordinary challenge.

The race into space

The following extract is from a speech given to a joint session of congress by President John F Kennedy on 25 May 1961. It introduced the extraordinary project to get a man on the moon. I've added comments in brackets to highlight how this is a really well-constructed objective statement:

> First, I believe that this nation [who] should commit itself to achieving the goal, before this decade is out [when], of landing a man on the moon [where] and returning him safely to the earth [what/where]. No single space project in this period will be more impressive to mankind, or more important for the long-range exploration of space [why]; and none will be so difficult or expensive to accomplish. We propose to accelerate the development of the appropriate lunar space craft. We propose to develop alternate liquid and solid fuel boosters, much larger than any now being developed, until certain which is superior [how – technical]. We propose additional funds for other engine development and for unmanned explorations [how – financial] – explorations which are particularly important for one purpose which this nation will never overlook: the survival of the man who first makes this daring flight. But in a very real sense, it will not be one man going to the moon – if we make this judgement affirmatively, it will be an entire nation. For all of us must work to put him there [who].

This was part of a historic speech and was a brilliant objective that culminated in the successful return of the Apollo 11 crew after the first walk on the moon.

You now have a choice of different frameworks to construct a good set of objectives for your project. Using one or more of the models, you can also review an objective to check that all the necessary information has been included.

Objectives: summary and actions

1. Hold a workshop with appropriate stakeholders in the project to ensure you have a picture of the expectations of the different parties that is as complete as possible. This *must* include the views of the customer/s for the project – whether they are within the company or external. They are the ones who want the project and their wishes must be understood. This may be a direct representative of the customer or someone from your marketing team. Whichever way you do it, you need to have the 'voice of the customer'.

2. Work with the group, and with any information provided to you, to structure a draft objective statement for the project that answers the following questions:
   - **Where** are we and **why** are we doing this project?
   - **What** are we going to do?
   - **How** will we do it and **who** will do it?
   - **How** will we know when it's done?
   - **What** will we do next?

3. Review the draft objective statement you've created against the SMART criteria and amend as necessary, or identify further investigation to establish the ability to succeed with the project.

4. Discuss the draft project objectives offline with rest of the project team and any experts necessary to confirm the project viability (technically, financially, in terms of the market, etc). Amend as necessary.

5. Review the project objective with the customer and other stakeholders. Make any changes and establish when you have agreement from all.

6. Issue the project objectives as a formal document to the stakeholders and project team. This will form the basis for creating the plan, business case, milestones, etc.

Note. On bigger projects, you should add an issue number to the document. If you need to change the objective document it should be reissued and the version number changed. In this case, the amended version should indicate the changes from the previous version, the date this occurred and who authorized those changes.

7

Milestones

One of the most important yet misunderstood and misused concepts in project management is the milestone. Milestones are a vital part of creating the precision and shared understanding that are needed for a successful project.

Let's consider a project made up of a number of different, overlapping modules of work. The most serious problems often occur at the boundaries between these different elements. Unless the interfaces are defined clearly the project is unlikely to unfold as you expect and, just like the Mars Orbiter, it may crash and burn into oblivion.

 A milestone must be a specific, measurable, state of achievement within the project.

To understand the importance of well-defined milestones, it is useful to think about some poor milestones first.

THE PROBLEM WITH BAD MILESTONES

The main culprit for poor milestones is software like Microsoft Project. OK, so the culprit is the person hitting the keys, but Project lets you check a box against any task and instantly it is marked by a black diamond that indicates it's a milestone. Don't be fooled. A group of black pixels doesn't magically convert a task into a clear and unambiguous milestone. The following example will illustrate this.

Consider a project where a new manufacturing plant is being built from scratch and production started. One of the milestones could be as follows:

Milestone: Deliver injection moulding machine to factory.

Let's be charitable and assume it's the right machine. At a review meeting everyone has been told that the milestone is complete. However, the machine is actually still packed up in a container outside the factory and the production team are not exactly pleased.

So is the next version better?

Milestone: Deliver and install injection moulding machine in factory.

Again, you can meet that milestone but the machine has not been set up to run. Installation may only mean it has just been bolted to the floor.

Before the machine can be used, it needs compressed air and an electricity supply. Will meeting the following milestone satisfy the production team?

Milestone: Deliver injection moulding machine to factory and install/fix services.

Are you nodding your head now? Even a bit? What else is there to worry about?

If you go to speak to the production engineers and ask them what is required to begin production with an injection moulding machine they'll tell you. There is probably a test batch that has to be put through the machine and the pieces produced and then checked for quality and consistency. Only at the satisfactory completion of this process can the machine be used for production.

Hopefully you can see how a poorly defined milestone can lead to all kinds of problems and misunderstandings.

HOW TO WRITE A GOOD MILESTONE

A milestone should not be about doing something: it should be about having arrived somewhere. It's a place in the project that is unambiguous and clear to all in terms of what is meant when it has been achieved. Milestones, along with objectives, are an excellent way to identify misunderstandings before the project starts and eliminate those nasty surprises.

When the two railway tracks meet in the middle of the country you want to make sure they have the same width between the tracks. The Channel Tunnel was dug from both sides of the English Channel and the constructors were very keen to make sure these tunnels met up (even though they would have had twice the number of tunnels to use otherwise).

You need to find issues early and fix the problems and potential misunderstandings before they become crises at a point when it's too late to fix them.

Milestones need to be states of achievement

Imagine you are on a journey and need to travel to New York on 22 June. Let's compare two milestone statements for that journey.

Milestone 1: Take flight BA64 from Heathrow Airport to New York on 22 June this year.

That is a very specific statement and it's measurable for sure. You can tick off that you get that flight and so the milestone is fine, right?

Well what happens if the flight is diverted? What happens if you board it but it can't depart because of a problem? You will have achieved the milestone you defined but gone nowhere!

Let's try another version.

Milestone 2: Be in New York City (United States) on 22 June this year and standing at the top of the Empire State Building.

Can you see any ambiguity with that milestone? If that is ticked off then it can only be on that day, and before the Empire State Building has closed, that you are there in New York City!

Let's consider a different example:

- Would you want a milestone in your project where someone has to 'programme a new database for six weeks'?
- What happens if the software is not complete after the six weeks?
- What happens if it doesn't work at all or has bugs?

The emphasis has to again shift from performing an action (programming in this case) to having achieved something tangible. The milestone for this should be something more like:

Milestone: The milestone is complete when the new module is completed and has passed the test protocol defined by the client in document xx.

Concentrating on where you need to be rather than how you get there gives you enormous clarity and flexibility in a project.

In the case of going to New York, you could skate, swim, walk, row, fly, sail, run, ride, cycle, etc to get there. It's not about the getting there – it's about being somewhere.

In the case of the software module you could have it written in-house by employees, use sub-contractors, use external software houses, buy in open source code, etc. The testing could again be in-house or turned over to a third-party software testing company.

Around the world in 80 days

Phineas Fogg did not define every part of his route as he went around the world. He had flexibility because it was not about the way the journey should take place; it was just about being back in the Reform Club on a particular day.

WRITING MILESTONES

Milestones should be:

- Phrased around a specific outcome rather than a set of activities. Remember, it is about being somewhere rather than the journey itself.
- Measurable – some part of the milestone should be a statement of the evidence that the milestone has been reached.
- Used to indicate important decision points or achievements on the way to the overall project objective.
- Limited to around 10–15 per project or plan – although each milestone can have its own smaller, sub-milestones that contribute to achieving it. As project manager, you are looking for significant, top-level milestones that relate to the decisive points in the project.

To write a good milestone statement, you can use the following structure:

'The milestone is complete when' **<state of achievement>** and **<measure of quality>**.
The **state of achievement** – this is where you define where the project should be when the milestone is complete.
The **measure of quality** – this is how you will know that the milestone has been met to the appropriate quality.

Table 7.1 shows some examples of milestone statements put together using this syntax.

DIFFERENCES BETWEEN MILESTONES AND GATES

In some organizations, confusion occurs because they are running a process to assess projects at different points in their lifecycle. It is worth explaining why these processes are used, how they work and how they complement, but do not replace, the milestones on a project.

Table 7.1 Some examples of milestone statements

The milestone is complete when…

State of achievement	and	Quality statement
The draft specification is complete	and	has been signed off by the Director of Design
The G12 processor batch test is complete	and	the rate passing the Acceptance Test Protocol exceeds 99.999%
The first 200 customers have been acquired, provided with service	and	the monitoring software confirms that all have transferred at least one megabyte of information over the network

Why gate processes are needed

A major problem in a project can be securing management approval to continue. To provide a consistent way of progressing a portfolio of projects, Cooper developed the widely used 'stage gate'™ process. It is important to understand the differences between specific project milestones and generic 'gates' within processes.

A critical problem and delay in projects occurs where you are six weeks from the next senior team meeting and are waiting for them to make a decision. It is worse when your project issues get bumped from that agenda and you are then waiting for the following meeting (and that is infuriatingly frequent, I can assure you).

To minimize delays in decision making and also reduce the need for senior management input, the 'stage gate'™ approach introduces specific criteria that must be met for a project to proceed. This means that the intentions of senior management are captured in the criteria and so it is no longer necessary to have them meet up to discuss every individual project. Other people can review the project, assess if the particular criteria for that step in the project's life have been met and then give the go or no-go for the project to continue without any of the delays. This approach also removes much of

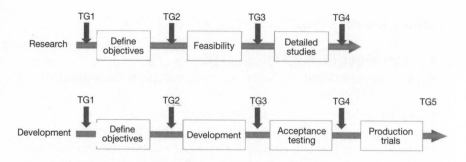

Figure 7.1 Example gate processes for research and development

the uncertainty and inconsistency in decision making, as everyone understands both the process and the criteria in advance.

To illustrate this better, it is worth looking more closely at 'gates' and then comparing them with milestones so that you can understand the important differences. Figure 7.1 shows examples of both a research and a development-style gate process.

At any of the toll gate (TG) points, there is a list of criteria that need to be met in order for the project to continue. Figure 7.1 shows how research projects have different generic stages in their life compared to development projects. They will also have different criteria applied at the decision points. At these points, the individual project will be reviewed against a set of criteria that evaluate different things (eg forecast return on investment, client acceptance of objectives, marketing agreement, completion of business case).

Now let's compare gates and milestones to highlight the differences.

Gates

- **Are generic** – they apply to **every** project of a particular type, eg research, construction.
- **Have a common set of criteria** imposed on all projects of a given type.
- **Represent key review pointss** against predefined criteria.
- Projects may be stopped or put on hold at a gate review even if they could successfully achieve their objectives.

Milestones

- Are **unique** to each individual project.
- Failure to achieve a milestone will result in the project being cancelled or put on hold – even if they would otherwise pass every gate.

Hopefully you can see that milestones are about the performance of the project in achieving the defined objectives, whereas gates are about the fit of a project to a business (eg return on investment, or fit with current strategy).

To succeed, a project will have to achieve all its milestones and pass every review point (gate), as shown in Figure 7.2.

I like gate processes, but if they are not well applied they will not protect you from cost over-runs and delays, as the following example about the defence industry illustrates.

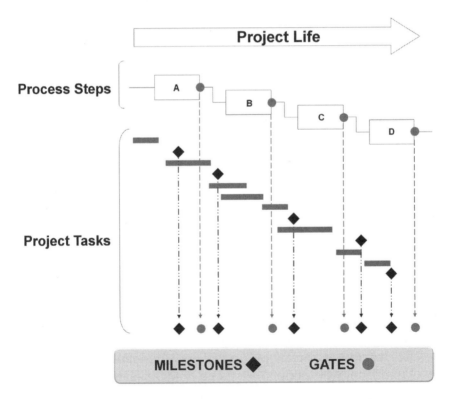

Figure 7.2 The relationship between gates and milestones

In 2003, the National Audit Office (NAO) in the UK looked at 18 major defence programmes and identified an average time over-run per programme of 18 months, and cost over-runs of £3 billion (US $5.5 billion).

At that time, performance was actually improving due to 'smart-acquisition' practices and the imposition of a detailed gate-style process. Four legacy projects, dating from before the new approach was implemented, were responsible for much of the delay. However, there was still concern that some projects were passing the main approval 'gate' with too much risk remaining in the project and an insufficient understanding of the maturity of the projects.

The impact of this was seen two years later in a subsequent NAO report when this flawed implementation of the improved processes meant there was little improvement.

In 2005, the 20 largest projects that had passed the main gate approval had an average time over-run of 20 months (excluding the Joint Strike Fighter), and cost over-runs of £2.7 billion (10 per cent of the approved budget).

Milestones: summary and actions

1. Work with the project team and customer to identify a potential list of important milestones between the start and finish of the project. Don't worry about how many milestones are generated by the team at this point. Let the team members keep working until they run out of steam.
2. Cut the list down to the 10 to15 that indicate the most important decision points or achievements on the way to completing the overall project.
3. Write statements for each milestone that are phrased around a specific **outcome** rather than a set of **activities** and that are measurable – some part of the milestone should be a statement of the evidence that the milestone has been reached. The syntax for each milestone statement should be:

'The milestone is complete when' <state of achievement> and <measure of quality>.

4. Review the milestones with the project team and identify any questions that cannot be resolved immediately but which need clarification eg 'How will we know when this milestone is complete?'
5. Assemble the initial milestone list and amend as necessary when outstanding information is provided.
6. Develop appropriate sub-milestones for the upcoming phases of the project.

8

Refining Milestones

DO YOU HAVE THE RIGHT MILESTONES?

One limitation of milestones is that although they may make sense individually, they may fail to adequately represent the complete project when taken as a whole. It can also be tricky to understand how they fit together relative to one another.

One approach to check the milestones you have created is based on a process mapping technique called 'swim lanes'. This places the steps in a process into different lanes according to who performs them or what type of activity they are.

HOW RESULT PATHS HELP

Result paths divide the milestones into different categories of the project and then connect them to show you the sequencing and split of milestones between the categories; see Figure 8.1.

This approach can help by:

- showing the route the milestones create between different categories – illustrating where there will be handovers to manage;

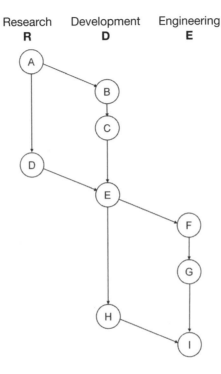

Figure 8.1 A milestone result path

- showing the distribution of the milestones between the different categories – showing where more milestones might be necessary;
- enabling the team to order the milestones and sub-milestones beneath them.

SETTING UP RESULT PATHS

Deciding on categories

To create a results path for the milestones, you need to select three categories. There is no formula for deciding which categories to use. In fact, it can be very useful to think imaginatively about which categories to try. Here are some more obvious combinations:

Marketing/Finance/Production
Research/Engineering/Development
Design/Test/Quality
Implementation/Site Engineering/Client Acceptance

You may find thinking more laterally also provides useful information, eg Internal/External/Client.

Creating the result paths

To create the result path you need to group the milestones by category. This gives you three lists, as shown in Figure 8.2.

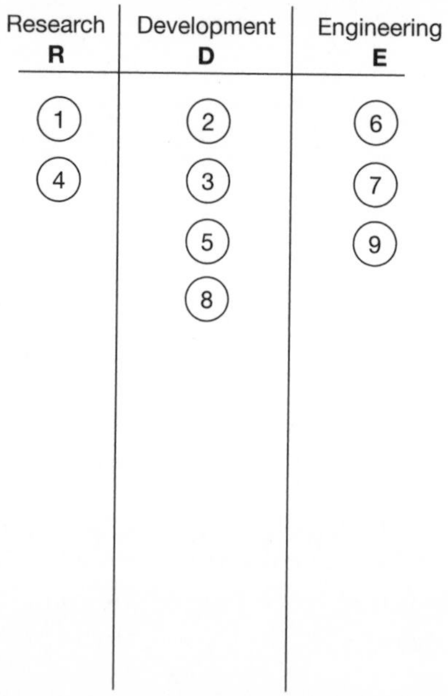

Figure 8.2 Milestones in categories

You then need to consider the relationship between the milestones. It may not always be clear what the exact relationship is but you should start by thinking about roughly when they occur in the life of the project in relation to one another – which milestone comes first, which one is next, etc.

This will help provide an impression of the overall 'shape' of the project. Figure 8.3 shows the milestones roughly in time order (the start of the project at the top of the page, with time running down the page).

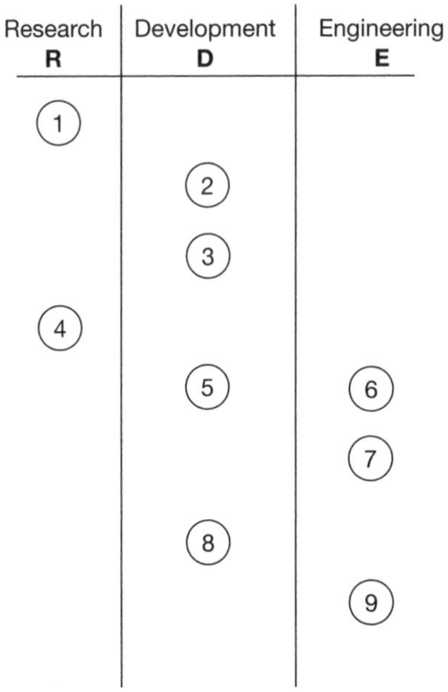

Figure 8.3 Milestones in categories and ordered over the life of the project

The final step is to draw in the relationships between the milestones. Again these are not going to be part of the plan; they are just there to illustrate relationships so that you can improve the milestones for the project.

ASSESSING RESULT PATHS

When you have created the result paths, you can then start to think about what you can learn from them. Consider the example in Figure 8.5.

PROJECT NAME: New US01 Production Facility				**DATE: 17 May**

DATE	Research R	Development D	Engineering E	Milestone Statements
17 May	R1			**R1** is complete when **<state of achievement>** and **<measure of quality>**.
4 Jun		D1		**D1** is complete when **<state of achievement>** and **<measure of quality>**.
15 Jul		D2		**D2** is complete when **<state of achievement>** and **<measure of quality>**.
6 Aug	R2			**R2** is complete when **<state of achievement>** and **<measure of quality>**.
28 Aug		D3		**D3** is complete when **<state of achievement>** and **<measure of quality>**.
15 Sep			E1	**E1** is complete when **<state of achievement>** and **<measure of quality>**.
21 Sep			E2	**E2** is complete when **<state of achievement>** and **<measure of quality>**.
10 Oct		D4		**D4** is complete when **<state of achievement>** and **<measure of quality>**.
25 Oct			E3	**E3** is complete when **<state of achievement>** and **<measure of quality>**.

Figure 8.4 Result paths with milestone statements

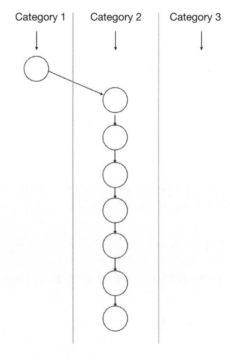

Figure 8.5 Example result path

Why is there no milestone in the third category? This may not be a problem, depending on the categories you have selected, but you should at least ask yourself why.

Now let's look at same project using three different categories; see Figure 8.6.

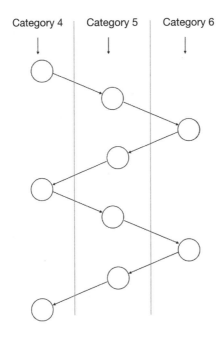

Figure 8.6 Example result path

This project switches from one category to another repeatedly. This shows that you need to pay extra attention at the interfaces between these categories.

By looking at the same set of milestones with a few different sets of result paths you should either be reassured that you have the correct milestones, or understand that there are some omissions or amendments required.

DEVELOPING THE DETAIL FOR EACH MILESTONE

Milestones can be very significant pieces of work within a project and so warrant being structured using sub-milestones.

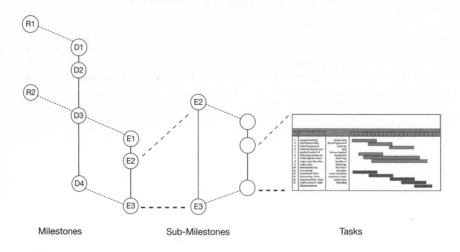

| Milestones | Sub-Milestones | Tasks |

Figure 8.7 How milestones, sub-milestones and tasks are related

In Figure 8.7, three sub-milestones are identified between milestone E2 and E3. These contribute to achieving milestone E3. Achieving a milestone (or a sub-milestone in this example) will be broken down into discrete tasks in the next chapter.

Sub-milestones should be written using the same structure used for the main milestones.

BEYOND MILESTONES

Once the milestones and/or sub-milestones for the project are defined, you can begin to create and structure a more detailed list of the tasks underneath. This becomes the work breakdown structure that will be discussed in the next chapter.

Refining milestones: summary and actions

1. Define three categories related to the project (departments, operations, phases, etc).
2. Group the project milestones by category.
3. Start to create a diagram of the relationships between the milestones over time (start to finish from top to bottom).

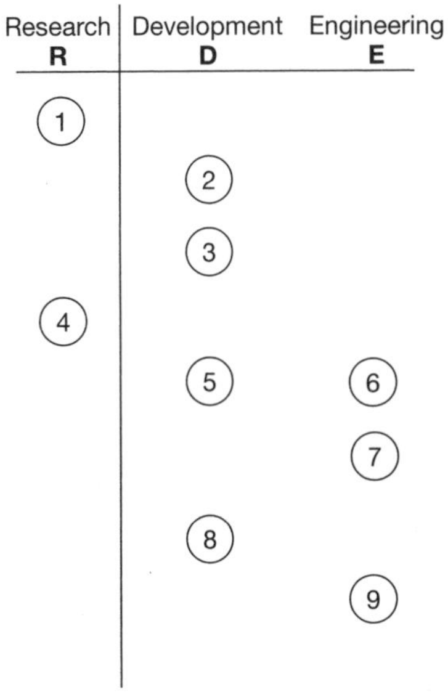

Research	Development	Engineering
R	**D**	**E**

①
　　②
　　③
④
　　⑤　　　⑥
　　　　　　⑦
　　⑧
　　　　　⑨

Figure 8.8 Milestones in categories and ordered over the life of the project

4. Map out the general relationships of the milestones, as shown in Figure 8.9.
5. Assess what you can learn from the result paths. Repeat steps 1–4 two or three more times and then amend the list of milestones as necessary.
6. Select the most appropriate categories and then issue a final result path to the project team along with the respective milestone statements (see Figure 8.10).
7. Develop and assess sub-milestones to detail the progress towards the major milestones in the project.

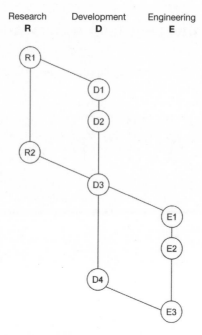

Figure 8.9 Result path diagram

DATE	Research R	Development D	Engineering E	Milestone Statements
PROJECT NAME: New US01 Production Facility				**DATE: 17 May**
17 May	R1			R1 is complete when <state of achievement> and <measure of quality>
4 Jun		D1		D1 is complete when <state of achievement> and <measure of quality>
15 Jul		D2		D2 is complete when <state of achievement> and <measure of quality>
6 Aug	R2			R2 is complete when <state of achievement> and <measure of quality>
28 Aug		D3		D3 is complete when <state of achievement> and <measure of quality>
15 Sep			E1	E1 is complete when <state of achievement> and <measure of quality>
21 Sep			E2	E2 is complete when <state of achievement> and <measure of quality>
10 Oct		D4		D4 is complete when <state of achievement> and <measure of quality>
25 Oct			E3	E3 is complete when <state of achievement> and <measure of quality>

Figure 8.10 Result paths with milestone statements

9

Activities/Work Breakdown Structure

So far in this book we have:

- considered the state of an ongoing project;
- looked at how to define a clear set of objectives;
- developed milestones (and sub-milestones) that mark important points of progress towards completion of the project.

Now we need to start creating detail in the work that will be done so that we can produce different scenarios for how long the project might take, the resources needed, etc.

The common element is that none of this requires you to touch a computer keyboard or look at a piece of project management software. Towards the end of this section you might consider starting to use software to capture the information. (You'll notice this is in stark contrast to people you may know who will start tapping at a keyboard at the first hint of a project.)

WHAT IS A WORK BREAKDOWN STRUCTURE?

 A work breakdown structure divides the project into progressively smaller pieces of work, allowing the project manager to assign the smaller work packages and tasks to resources.

If we think of a project to build a skyscraper, we could have parts of the project to do with foundations, structure, floors, walls and services. The foundations could involve surveying, digging, inserting piles and pouring foundations. The inserting piles work can be broken down into ground preparation, boring and insertion.

Each time we consider one part of the project we can then define the detail at the next level down; see Figure 9.1.

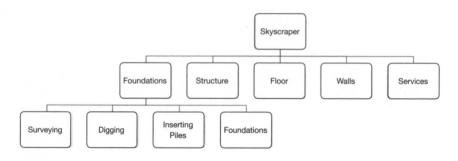

Figure 9.1 A work breakdown structure for constructing a building

The work breakdown structure divides the work into increasingly small chunks and allows you to relate those chunks to one another – knowing what pieces of work contribute to which larger section of the project.

The big chunks within a milestone – work packages

The project has milestones and these should be the start point for a work breakdown structure. The significant chunks of work contributing to the milestone are referred to as 'work packages', as they are a bundle of smaller tasks that can logically be considered in one grouping.

The work packages should also include pieces of work necessary to de-risk the project. Imagine that the third work package is very difficult technically, but there is an alternative approach that may also deliver the same results. This might be added in as an additional work package, as shown in Figure 9.2.

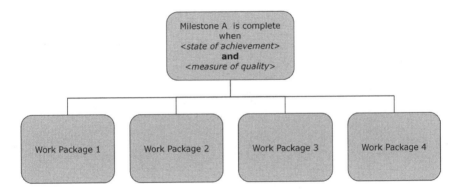

Figure 9.2 Additional work packages introduced to de-risk the milestone

To complete the milestone, Figure 9.3 shows that you need to complete work packages 1 and 2 and then either 3 or 4.

The detailed parts of a work package

Underneath each work package there will be progressively more detailed tasks/activities. Many pieces of project management software use a numbering system to make the hierarchical relationship between tasks clearer; see Figure 9.4.

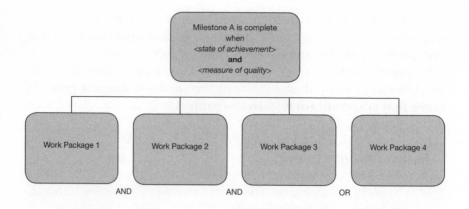

Figure 9.3 How the work packages are completed to deliver the milestone

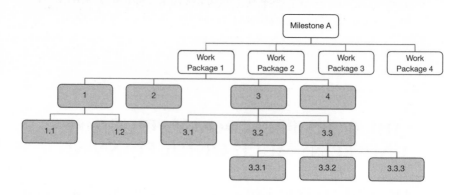

Figure 9.4 Numbering within a work breakdown structure

The tasks that make up task 3 are numbered 3.1, 3.2 and 3.3. The tasks that contribute to completing task 3.3 are numbered 3.3.1, 3.3.2, etc. In this way the task number allows you to see where a task sits within the overall project and how it relates to other tasks.

How small should a task be?

You could continue creating smaller and smaller tasks for ever, but there comes a point where common sense needs to kick in. There is generally no point in creating a task that is shorter than half a day to complete. This may seem an excessively high level of detail but important events, such as a board meeting, may only last half a day and yet be incredibly important for the project.

In simple terms, you continue breaking down the work into smaller elements until you arrive at **the smallest discrete piece of work that is significant within the project**.

Is this enough detail?

The head of a two-person group working to develop innovative carriers for wafer scale processors proudly showed me his plan. Lovingly created using PERT charts, the plan printed out as 24 A4 sheets for the next six months. I had to admit it was almost a masterpiece of modern art, but the level of detail was excessive for a two-person team and was planned in detail for far too long into the future.

Still, I kept that print-out for ages and would occasionally bring it out to scare people.

THE WORK BREAKDOWN STRUCTURE UNDERPINS MUCH OF THE PLANNING

When the work breakdown structure is in place, the project team has the information needed to:

- assign responsibilities within the team;
- allocate tasks to specific resources;
- estimate time against tasks to help understand the overall timing within the project;
- create a budget for the project;
- provide a structure for monitoring and reporting progress against budgets;
- predict spend to the end of the project/milestone;
- recognize and understand problems within the plan.

THE ROLLING WAVE APPROACH

When you are driving, you pay the most attention to the things that are closest to you. This makes sense as they are most likely to cause you problems (crash, swerve, stop) or provide you with information (signals, traffic lights, signs). You may give some of your attention to further up the road to get advance warning of traffic queues or other serious problems, but you are unlikely to give the horizon much more than a passing glance.

The same goes for projects. We don't need to plan five years in advance at enormous levels of detail. In most cases, projects will have a radically different set of circumstances five years out and your planning so far in advance will have been wasted. However, you do need more detail for the parts of the project that are closer to you.

Varying detail into the future

The main impacts of using a rolling wave approach are changes over time, in the level of detail provided for tasks and in the way you assign resources to tasks.

This means planning the project to the full level of task and resource detail for the next phase only. For the following phases, the planning should be less detailed and focus on securing scarce or key resources, as shown in Figure 9.5.

Figure 9.5 shows this decreasing level of detail on who does what as you look further into the future of the project.

The rolling wave of detail

As you progress through the life of the project, it is important to keep the same level of information in front of you. That's why the start of the previous diagram is labelled 'now'. You wouldn't take a look at the road in a car then close your eyes for the rest of your journey, and you don't do that with a project either.

The approach is called 'rolling wave' because you maintain the same level of detail and attention rolling in front of you as the project progresses.

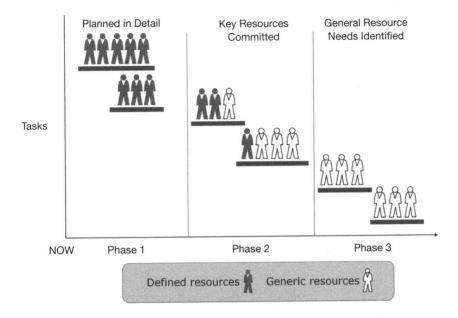

Figure 9.5 A rolling wave level of detail in planning

THE IMPACT OF ROLLING WAVE ON ESTIMATION AND CONTINGENCY

If the project is only planned in detail to the next milestone/gate then it is clear there will be a level of uncertainty in the exact budget required to complete the project. Part of this uncertainty relates to how the existing scope will be met and the rest is due to potential risks (risk-based contingency planning is discussed in more detail in Chapter 14).

In Figure 9.6, the actual cost of a project is shown over time. The 'base estimate to completion' is the estimate for the next phase/ milestone in detail and then budgetary estimates thereafter to get to the end of the project. As each phase is completed, the amount of the project remaining is reduced and so the base estimate will eventually trend to the actual project spend.

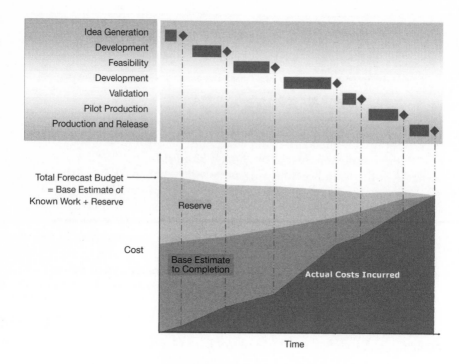

Figure 9.6 Base estimate of known work to completion plus reserve budget vs actual costs through the life of a project

The reserve figure represents additional budget added to the base estimate to take account of the uncertainty in the areas that remain unplanned in detail. This reserve is added to the base estimate to provide a total forecast budget for the project. As the project continues, the level of uncertainty reduces and so the reserve becomes a smaller percentage of the overall project spend.

This reserve could be as high as 100 per cent of the base estimate in software projects at the earliest stages, but reduces rapidly as the amount of work remaining falls and the level of understanding of the project increases.

Activities: summary and actions

To create an initial version of a work breakdown structure, the project manager should work with the team as follows:

1. Identify the milestone to be detailed.
2. Set up a whiteboard or flipchart with a Post-It note of the milestone statement placed on the left-hand side.
3. Ask the team how the milestone will be achieved – this should generate a list of possible work packages that can be captured on Post-Its. The reason I say 'possible' is that some will turn out to be smaller activities or duplicates
4. Collect the suggested work packages and position them to the right of the milestone.

    Remember that you should not just consider what needs to be done to complete the milestone but also consider what else could be done to de-risk the project. Include any additional work packages that provide alternative paths to a particular solution; see Figure 9.7.

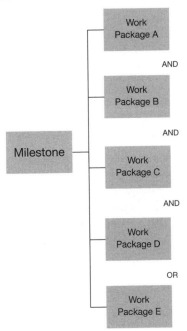

Figure 9.7 Breaking down a milestone into work packages with the team

5. For each work package, brainstorm the tasks that will be needed to complete it. Get the team to do this individually on Post-It notes.

6. Collect the notes and work with the team to remove any duplicates and then place the tasks on the whiteboard.

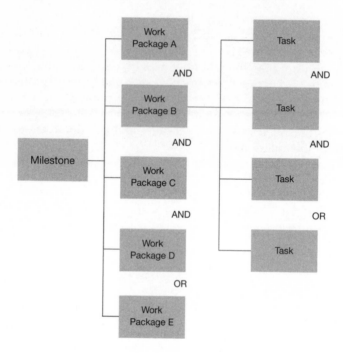

Figure 9.8 Defining tasks within work packages

7. Identify which tasks are actually sub-tasks and rearrange to place these to the right of the task they contribute to, as shown in Figure 9.9.

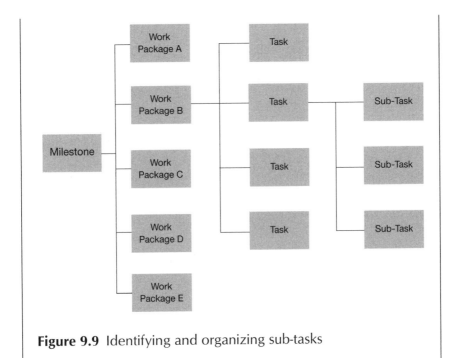

Figure 9.9 Identifying and organizing sub-tasks

10

Assigning Resources

Now that you have generated a detailed list of tasks for the project, the next stage is to assign resources to those tasks. The resources you need may be a specific person, machine or facility, or may be more generic, eg C++ programmers.

This is very important during the definition stage of the project when you are trying to understand the work involved and resources needed to complete each task. You will need to assign people to do this estimation work for you.

IDENTIFYING THE RESOURCES YOU NEED

If you have a choice, people who don't think about what they are doing and don't ask questions should not be on the team. Everyone needs to be fully involved in trying to do the best they can with their part of the project.

What the project doesn't need is people asleep at the wheel. Try to ensure you recruit the people who ask questions and have suggestions rather than those who just keep their heads down. The latter group may be easier to manage but they might let the project go over a cliff without either spotting it or letting you know – not a good result.

Assigning resources by role

To capture who is going to do what, you start with the task lists created previously. To show the different roles that individuals perform for a given task, you can use the following code letters:

A is available to Advise
C must be Consulted
d makes a decision with others
D makes a Decision alone
I should be Informed
P manages Progress
T provides Tuition
X eXecutes the work

These letters can be applied to a matrix showing the tasks and who performs what role, as in Figure 10.1.

This will then allow you to assign tasks and ensure that individuals understand who is involved when tasks are assigned to them. In particular, they know who can help them.

	Project Manager	Systems Manager	Client	Test Team	A. Mutrib	G. Murad
Create high level specification		A	I	C	X	
Develop unit test strategy					X	C
Define systems test strategy			I	X	C	A

Figure 10.1 Example assignment of resources by role

Contractors

Working with contractors is not a game of watching them fail from a distance. The project manager needs to actively help ensure any contractors or outside companies in the project succeed.

Contractors may not be employees of the company but they have the power to sink the project. The project manager should engage with them and ensure that they are committed to the project.

This engagement can be increased with an appropriate contract. The success of the project should be aligned with the rewards for the contractor. This might be a success fee element of payment or a penalty clause. However, you also need to work closely with them on a personal level. Make them feel part of the team wherever you can. Include them in social events and try to get them working on site with your team where possible. In simple terms, you want contractors to meld seamlessly with the rest of the project team. This means they will feel more peer pressure to succeed from within the team and are more likely to care about the objectives of the project.

Resources: summary and actions

To identify the resources needed to complete tasks, the project manager works with the team as follows:

1. Create a table of the tasks to be performed on paper, in Excel or by copying the task list from your project software into Excel or a Word table.
2. As you identify the people you need, add their name at the top of a new column for each.
3. In the column below their name, write in the role they perform for tasks that involve them by using the following code letters:
   - **A** is available to **A**dvise
   - **C** must be **C**onsulted
   - **d** makes a **d**ecision with others
   - **D** makes a **D**ecision alone
   - **I** should be **I**nformed

- **P** manages **P**rogress
- **T** provides **T**uition
- **X** e**X**ecutes the work
4. Where you do not have a name, write in the position within the project. You should end up with a table that looks like the one in Figure 10.2.

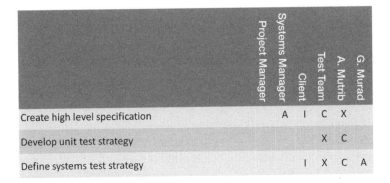

	Project Manager	Systems Manager	Client	Test Team	A. Mutrib	G. Murad
Create high level specification		A	I	C	X	
Develop unit test strategy					X	C
Define systems test strategy			I	X	C	A

Figure 10.2 Example assignment of resources by role

5. You now have the names and roles necessary to start estimating the duration of tasks within the project.

11

Time Estimation

Developing the work breakdown structure provides you with the information needed to estimate the duration of tasks. This is a critical area: the question everyone will keep asking is, 'When will the project be finished?'

When you start to work on estimating the time needed for tasks, you are going to hear some of the following: 'You can't plan R&D', 'It takes as long as it takes', and 'You can't plan software development.' In fact, what you are hearing is that the speaker just does not know how to estimate the work or that he or she has become so jaded by projects slipping that he or she despairs of estimating a task accurately.

Some things cannot be planned to the second. However, your job as project manager is to get the best possible view of how long something will take, even if there remains a high degree of uncertainty.

WHY ESTIMATION GOES WRONG

You can con someone into accepting a ridiculous deadline but you can't make them meet it.

There are a number of reasons why the estimates underpinning a project can be so badly wrong:

- blind over-confidence or padding by team members;
- different people estimate with different underlying assumptions;
- people who do the work were not involved in defining it;
- 'political' estimates – individuals or groups telling the project manager what they think they want to hear and not what is accurate;
- initial estimates are not updated realistically as the project proceeds.

To avoid these problems, you must ensure everyone on the team understands the approach to work content and estimation. If they either misunderstand or do not believe that you are going to play it straight with them, they will probably not deliver what you want.

The project update process will catch errors over time. Genuine errors can be put down to learning, but you need to eradicate errors through padding of estimates or from people providing 'political' answers.

Who should be involved in defining and estimating tasks?

The people doing the work must be involved in estimating it.

They are most important as they will be:

- executing the tasks;
- reporting back on progress;
- providing updated estimates on a regular basis.

It is vital that they believe, and are committed to, the estimates for the tasks they are working on. They may not always be capable of doing the estimation on their own but, as mentioned in Chapter

10, other people can be involved who may have the knowledge or experience necessary to help.

Dealing with the differences in how people estimate

When asked how long something will take, people will consider their current workload, holidays and the risks of the work they are being asked to do. They will factor in some extra time for contingencies (which will vary wildly from individual to individual) and generally let all these other factors 'mask' the actual time to do the work requested.

The approaches outlined later in this book will help you eliminate these problems.

Estimates need to be kept up to date

Initial estimates should be as accurate as is practical and sensible, but they will evolve over time as the project team learns more about tasks as they progress. This will normally translate into revisions of the amount of work that remains to complete the task but may also mean the task needs to be reassigned to a different resource.

Where initial estimates are not corrected over time, they create situations where the mismatch between the estimate and reality is only noticed when it is too late. By keeping estimates of work content up to date, you give yourself the chance to identify and resolve problems as early as possible.

WHY MANAGING USING 'PERCENTAGE COMPLETE' DOESN'T WORK

The first 90 per cent of a task will use 90 per cent of the resources assigned to it.

The last 10 per cent will use the other 90 per cent.

The point above may be humorous but it is based on bitter experience and is similar to what must be the biggest lie in project management.

'We're 95 per cent complete'

It's normally meant genuinely enough, but believing it is the biggest trap you can fall into. It seems pretty innocuous doesn't it? The problem is that it is almost always wrong. It's so badly wrong that you'll see experienced project managers who hear this phrase mutter '95 per cent to go!' under their breath in reply.

How can it be that someone working on a task can get it so wrong? The answer is simply that they are looking backwards in time rather than into the future. Let me explain what I mean.

How percentage complete is represented

In project management software, the length of time to complete a task is frequently displayed as a timeline. The length of the line is proportional to the expected duration of the task. Some may stretch over months, while others will be for just a day. This approach to looking at tasks within project is called a 'Gantt chart' and is discussed in Chapter 13.

The second line within the task bar shown in Figure 11.1 represents the percentage completion of the task. The length of the black bar is the same as the overall length of the task bar multiplied by the percentage complete. For example, the black bar will be half the

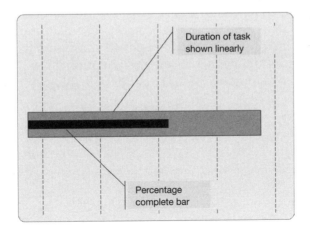

Figure 11.1 How a task is displayed as a timeline

length of the overall task bar in the case where the task is 50 per cent complete.

It's perfectly logical and a nice graphical representation of what you have achieved – however, it generally doesn't work!

How percentage complete reporting hides problems

The quality of the information used to calculate the percentage complete is the problem with the percentage complete approach.

Consider a task where someone provided an initial estimate of 20 days to complete the task. As work proceeds, they are regularly asked for the percentage complete. They will therefore be concentrating on two things: how much time they have spent to date, and the length of time they originally estimated.

The amount of time people spend on a task is important. You have a budget and people may be charged to the project in a variety of ways, so knowing the time spent is important. However, there are lots of people who can tell you what resources you have used on the project to date. There will be resource managers, cost centre managers, finance people all coming at you with numbers and pointing at particular figures with concern or delight. OK, I've never seen a finance person delighted but you get the point – this is an admin task and not the most important part of the project to get right. What is far more important to you is:

how far until we have finished the project?

The problems with percentage complete are that the people reporting on tasks fail to update the initial estimate for task duration, and are focused on the past (what has happened compared to the historic estimate) rather than concentrating on the future.

Let's use an everyday example to illustrate this point.

Imagine you are going for a walk and are unsure how far it is to the destination. You can see your end point, and you estimate it's around eight miles to get there. If I ask you about your progress and you used the percentage complete approach, you would try to figure out how far you have walked and then divide that into the eight miles. After a couple of miles walking you tell me you're

25 per cent of the way there. When you've measured out another two miles you say you're half way there.

Just think about it for a second: the one thing you're not doing is looking at the destination point. You are completely wrapped up in how far you have gone compared to your original, and frozen, estimate. If the destination was actually five miles or 25 miles away then your progress reports would be useless.

This problem is particularly damaging in projects. When things turn out differently from how you expect, you end up with surprises late on in the project, when you can't rescue the situation.

This error mechanism is how the effect of '95 per cent complete' occurs. Someone has been reporting progress as percentage complete and arrives at 95 per cent one week. They don't complete the task in the next week either. They look at their original estimate and see they have exceeded the amount of time estimated at the start of the task, so what can they do? Reporting 105 per cent complete is obviously nonsensical, so they just freeze their estimate, like a 39-year old avoiding the big 4-0! Week after week the task sticks at 95 per cent and, in reality, you have no idea how bad things really are because nothing has compelled the person to revise his or her estimate and consider what is left to do!

The right question – how far is there to go?

For the person taking the walk in the example above, and the person working on a project, there is a simpler question to ask: 'How far is there to go?'

That way we are tracking one simple but important variable. Instead of looking back and using an out-of-date estimate, the team is looking forward and considering what needs to be done to complete the task, and issues will be identified, and hence resolved, far earlier during the project.

This is an important principle that will be built on in the rest of the chapter. However, it is important to look at the topic of estimation first.

A BETTER APPROACH FOR ESTIMATION – WORK CONTENT

It's not the time, it's the work that matters

To begin with, let's define task duration as **the elapsed length of time it will take to complete a given task**. We need to get to a task duration and there are some ways of deriving durations that work and some that don't.

There are a couple of major problems with durations provided by team members.

- They are often unaware of the differences between their own approach to estimation and the approach taken by other members of the team. They don't know if they should add some contingency time or not. If they do add some, should it be 10 per cent, 50 per cent or 100 per cent?
- The durations are based on their own availability at that point in time. If the project slips then their availability will have changed and the estimated durations will no longer be valid.

Consider an example. A team member is about to go on a course for two weeks when you ask them to complete a task. They know the task will only take a couple of hours. They are literally walking out of the door when you ask how long to finish the task. Perfectly reasonably, they tell you it will be two weeks (not because it requires two weeks of effort but because they are away for that long).

The duration estimate won't be valid when the person returns from the course. If you ask them as they arrive back, they might say two hours. Even if you asked someone to estimate a task duration some time in the future it will always be susceptible to error when the task moves forward or back in the schedule and is impacted by other things they have to do.

In addition, problems crop up when you try to change who carries out this task. The information saying the task would take two weeks to carry out is of no use whatsoever if someone else is to do the work. The estimated duration for the task relates entirely to the availability of the first person you asked. You can assign the task to someone else and put two weeks duration next to it in your plan, but that won't relate accurately to the new person's situation.

They may be available to complete the task immediately or it may take them even longer!

This task duration estimate is pretty useless in the real world. The estimated time to complete the job has been completely distorted by the availability of the person to work on the task at the moment you asked them.

Hopefully you can appreciate that you cannot allocate tasks from one person to another if their estimates are created by other team members based on their own availability.

What is work content?

 Work content is the amount of time it would take for someone to complete a task if they were working from 9 to 5 without interruptions from other projects, meetings, discussions, holidays, training, etc.

Defining the pure work content of a task is a way to strip away all the subjective areas where people can pad or mask the true amount of work to be done.

OK – but all these interruptions are real, right? Can you ignore them and just estimate the amount of time if someone had 'perfect days'. Actually that is precisely what you want from the team! However, you must make sure the team both understands the concept clearly and trusts you. The last point cannot be overstated. The team **has** to trust you if they are going to give you accurate estimates of pure work content.

Think about it. When they were asked for the duration for a task in the past, they were totally in control. They could add in their comfort factors, some padding to allow for things going wrong and ensure they have enough time included to meet all their other responsibilities. Essentially they can give themselves as much slack in durations as their own aversion to failure demands.

In contrast, the work content approach is stripped bare. The key to success is that you must explain the work content approach to the team and reassure them that the real availability of each person will be used to calculate the overall task duration. This process will map the work content estimates onto each team member's real situation (availability, training, holidays, other projects, etc) to create realistic durations for tasks.

If the team don't trust you, they may be concerned that it's a scam to commit them to hideously short times to finish their tasks. This is why clarity in what you are doing and the trust of the team are absolutely vital. This trust can be built up as the team sees you doing what you have said you will.

In the real world you may get people who continue to try to keep their comfortable padded durations for tasks, but if you can spot them, you need to ramp up the pressure to get them working as you require.

PRODUCING GOOD ESTIMATES

Let's assume that the team members understand that they need to deliver accurate estimates of work content. The problem remains that they may not have the experience or knowledge to deliver the estimate that is needed. In this case there are a few different approaches that can help team.

Simple techniques

Ask inexperienced team members to find help in producing a good estimate or find that help yourself – that's your job as project manager.

Assess the results of previous projects. What happened last time? Who did this type of work before? What can be learnt from them?

More complex estimation

Some tasks have a range of possible durations. These can be harder to deal with as you're not sure which estimate to work with. Do you use the most optimistic estimate and hope for the best, or go with the most pessimistic and accept you are probably being over-cautious?

The answer is, as you may have guessed, a trade-off. Let's use a real example to illustrate the approach.

A medical company needed moulds for manufacturing a new inhaler for asthmatics. The history of making these moulds showed that on one occasion it had taken only one cycle of rework to get the size of the moulded parts correct. However, another time it took 16 attempts! Each rework cycle would take a week and so the potential variation of delivering this critical piece of equipment was almost four months!

That is an extreme example, but you will often be faced by similar situations where there is potentially a wide variance in the duration for a task. One way to approach this problem is to ask the team for three different estimates of the duration:

1. Optimistic duration – assuming things go well.
2. Pessimistic duration – assuming things go badly.
3. Most probable duration (expected) – the duration you'd bet on being correct.

Figure 11.2 shows how the work content of a project varies depending on which type of estimate you use.

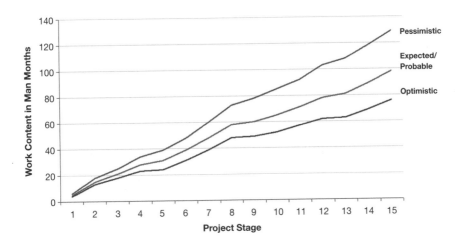

Figure 11.2 Different estimation methods and their impact on cumulative work estimates

We know an **expected** or **most probable** estimate is the duration that will happen most frequently for a given task. The optimistic and pessimistic results will occur less often.

The approach to combine the estimates together is to give more emphasis to the most probable result. This can be done with the following formula that creates an estimate that is weighted towards the most probable figure but takes account of the other values:

$$\text{Estimate} = \frac{\text{optimistic} + \text{pessimistic} + 4 \times (\text{most probable})}{6}$$

This is relatively simple and should work fine in most projects. However, if you have better information, you can adjust the weightings between the different duration estimates.

For example, imagine you had seen the results shown in Table 11.1.

Table 11.1 Example results

Weeks of modelling needed to complete evaluation	Times you have seen this result
1	1
4	20
10	2
Total	23 results/cases

This gives me a most optimistic duration of one week, a pessimistic duration of 10 weeks and a most probable duration of four weeks. The probable duration is clear from the table as it occurs far more often than the others.

There are now three estimates, and the three weightings to use with them are the number of times these events occur. However, the number that you use on the bottom of the calculation is not 6 anymore. That was used because you had 6 times the durations on the top line (1 × pessimistic, 1 × optimistic and 4 × probable). In this example you have 23 different cases you are taking into account (1 × optimistic, 2 × pessimistic and 20 × probable). The same logic applies though, so the calculation would divide the sum of the durations seen previously by the number of estimates on the top row:

$$\text{Estimate} = \frac{1 \times \text{optimistic} + 2 \times \text{pessimistic} + 20 \times (\text{most probable})}{23}$$

The more general case is:

$$\text{Estimate} = \frac{(\text{opt. events} \times \text{opt. dur.}) + (\text{pess. events} \times \text{pess. dur.}) + (\text{most prob. events} \times \text{most prob. dur.})}{\text{Total number of events (opt.} + \text{pess.} + \text{most probable)}}$$

Software packages such as Microsoft Project allow you to enter the three duration estimates and will do this calculation for you. In addition, these packages allow you to change the 'weightings' for the three types of estimate if necessary.

RECORD ANY ASSUMPTIONS USED IN ESTIMATION

It is vital that any assumptions made during the estimation process are recorded. It is very easy to forget but some estimates may be:

- based on provisional information;
- waiting for the results of a feasibility study;
- reliant on a senior management decision.

By maintaining a list of the assumptions, the project manager knows the estimates he or she can rely on and the ones that will need improvement and/or confirmation later on. In addition, you should ensure that assumptions with potentially controversial implications are circulated and approved by senior management, the customer etc.

The task durations can be calculated when you combine the work content estimates you have for tasks with the availability of resources The next chapter will show how to define the real availability of resources.

Time estimation: summary and actions

Inform the team involved in estimation that you are using an approach that focuses on concepts that are probably new to them and will require some explanation/training from you.

1. To remove the errors and misunderstandings that occur when people estimate the elapsed time to complete a task, the project will concentrate on work content instead.
    Work content is the amount of time it would take for someone to complete a task at their desk from 9 to 5 without interruptions from other projects, meetings, discussions, holidays, training, etc.

2. Ask members of the team to provide estimates for the work content of project tasks. This should always be the work content required to complete the task from now and not based on percentage complete, etc.

3. Where team members do not have the right experience or knowledge to carry out estimation, ensure they:
    –   find help for the estimation;
    –   review the results of previous projects within the company;
    –   look outside the company for the relevant information (internet, trade journals, independent experts, etc).

4. For tasks that are more complex to estimate accurately, or that are particularly at risk of overrunning, ask the team to produce optimistic, probable and pessimistic work content estimates for the particular task.

5. A general formula can be applied to the different estimates, for example:

$$\text{Estimate} = \frac{\text{optimistic} + \text{pessimistic} + 4 \times (\text{most probable})}{6}$$

6. If you have historical information then use this to create a more accurate estimate for the work content of a future task based on previous results:

$$\text{Estimate} = \frac{(\text{opt. events} \times \text{opt. dur.}) + (\text{pess. events} \times \text{pess. dur.}) + (\text{most prob. events} \times \text{most prob. dur.})}{\text{Total number of events (opt. + pess. + most probable)}}$$

7. Use spreadsheets or project management software to do these complex estimates of work content.
8. Circulate the estimates for review among the team and further discussion and/or correction where necessary.
9. Create an assumptions list and record and plan any further actions necessary to improve the estimates.

12

Resource Availability

Once you have estimates for the work content of a task, you need to understand the real availability of the resources to be able to calculate how long each task will take in practice.

ESTIMATING TASK DURATIONS FROM THE WORK CONTENT

There are two approaches you can use to convert work content estimates into actual task durations.

The first is useful for where you have a large team of broadly similar resources working on a task and you want a quick and dirty duration estimate. In this case you can apply a general availability factor across the group.

The second is where you need to use the availability for each individual to produce more accurate estimates.

Large teams

This approach uses averaged figures for availability that suggest:

- 10 per cent of overall time will be lost to holidays;
- 20 per cent of overall time will be lost to distractions (interruptions, coffee, chatting, cyber-slacking, etc);
- 70 per cent of overall time will be available to work on activities.

To derive how long a task will take for this group you could apply the following formula:

$$\text{Duration for task} = \frac{\text{Work content (days)}}{0.7 \text{ (availability)} \times \text{Full Time Equivalents committed}}$$

So a task with work content of 100 person-days with 10 people working on it will apparently have a task duration of just over 14 days.

You could also use this approach as a quick rule of thumb estimate for how long tasks may take. However, I would advise against it. This is a very coarse estimate and experience has shown that when senior teams and customers hear an estimate they cling on to it, integrate it into their presentations and attach their careers to it in ways that make it very difficult to change later.

If you do amend things later then you may get flak for any changes you make that worsen the situation. Remember, embarrassing senior management is rarely a good idea. They have means, motive and ample opportunities to pay you back.

To summarize – don't let any estimates based on this approach get anywhere near the project sponsor, steering committee, etc.

Understanding the commitments of resources

With a big team and a long task, the effect of events such as holidays, training, etc may not seem particularly significant as long as there is time in the plan to allow for them. However, let's think of a project where you have a key individual about to deliver the critical part of the project. When you go to see her you find she has just gone on holiday for two weeks! You might have made allowance for her taking a break, but you didn't want her to do it now!

For most people in the team, you **do need to understand the exact availability** because, as just described, it can have a critical impact on the project.

What basis are members of the team starting from in estimating their availability? How many hours do they start with in a week? Are they supposed to work 40, 37.5 or something else? This is a tricky area because many people work beyond their contracted hours. Depending on the circumstances you can use their contract hours or the hours they more normally work (which could well be nearer to 50). The reason I say it is tricky is that someone might tell you they work 50 hours a week but to plan for them to do that is sometimes illegal or may simply make you look like a slave-driver. Their extra hours are 'volunteered' by them but are not yours to use as a right.

You will need to make a decision on this depending on the particular project. Discuss with team members what the right figure to use for them should be. Using their contracted hours will, at worst, be an underestimate of their actual hours and will give you some spare time in hand.

Once you have established individuals' baseline hours each week, you then look at the regular non-project tasks they are doing. An example is shown in Table 12.1 (assuming a 40-hour week in this case). The total available for that person to work on moving the project forward is **only 17 hours a week**!

Sadly, during those 17 hours he will not be productive all the time. In fact, he will still be interrupted, take calls, get coffee, chat, etc. So you need to apply that 20 per cent factor here to show that he

Table 12.1 Estimating time spent on non-project tasks

Regular activities	Mon	Tues	Wed	Thurs	Fri
Team meetings	2	1	1	1	1
Briefing	1			1	1
Training	1				
Liaison meetings			2	3	3
HR		1			2
Miscellaneous	1				1
Available	**3**	**6**	**5**	**3**	**0**

will only be able to progress your tasks for (17 × 80 per cent) = **13.6 hours a week!**

That is a huge difference compared to the case where project managers assume you'll get 40 hours progress from each team member each week. First of all these managers are deluded and then they are fired (normally in that order).

Managing the impact of holidays and sudden changes in availability

We have seen the effect of regular tasks and interruptions in diminishing time available to work on the project.

To plan for these automatically, you can use the 'calendar' functions of planning software. This means you can adjust the real availability of a specific resource (person, machine, etc) to reflect the amount of time they are available and also block out time when they are away on holiday, training, etc.

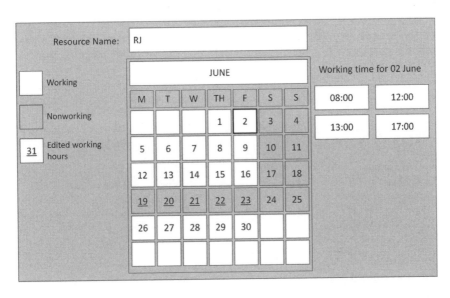

Figure 12.1 Example calendar for a resource with 'typical' availability

The calendar view in Figure 12.1 shows RJ working a 40-hour week. He is shown as working from 08:00 to 12:00 and then from 13:00 to 17:00. We're not worried about the lunchtimes, but the overall result is that this person is down for an eight-hour day.

A simple approach to using calendars is to divide the weekly time a person has available to work on the project into five days and then tweak the time the calendar shows them as working to match their actual available hours.

In Figure 12.2, RJ's working time has been reduced to reflect the time he can usefully contribute to the project – four hours each day. This has been done by changing the hours worked to only be from 08:00 to 12:00.

When a resource is assigned a task, the software will use the duration you have estimated (as discussed before) and calculate how long it will *really* take to complete using the resource's actual availability that you set in the software.

- A 100-hour task for someone available only 25 hours a week will therefore spread over four weeks;
- A 20-hour task for a test facility that is only available two hours a week will spread over 10 weeks.

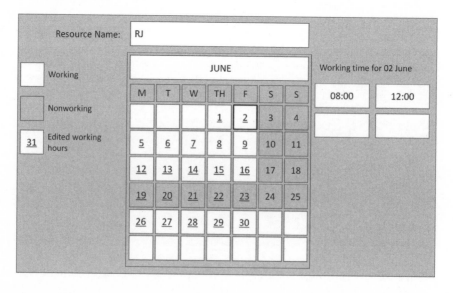

Figure 12.2 Example calendar for a resource with reduced availability

However, this approach has still not taken account of exceptional absences at this point. By that I mean holidays, seminars, training courses and other periods where the person may be away for some time. Using the same calendar feature in the software, you can block out the time for these events as being 'non-working' for that particular person. The software will again adjust the overall task duration to reflect this by spreading tasks so that they run across the absence.

- A 100-hour task for someone available 25 hours a week, and with two weeks holiday will therefore spread over six weeks.
- A 20-hour task for a test facility available two hours a week and with a four-week maintenance shutdown will spread over 14 weeks.

You can do all these calculations on paper but there comes a point where you should use the tools available. It is important to stay away from the computer when you are planning the objectives, milestones and initial work breakdown as you want people focused on the process and not mindlessly tapping away before they have thought through what the project is trying to achieve. However, the software can save you huge amounts of time as you start to plan the detailed execution of the project and as tasks are moved around in time.

Having a dedicated calendar is equally valid for technical resources and equipment, eg an electron microscope or a pilot production facility. These resources can't talk for themselves (if they do, it's a sign you're working too hard!). However, there should be a schedule that you can check and on which you can book time for using the resources.

'Crashing' the project – sometimes adding more people slows you down

Crashing is the process of adding more resources to a task in an effort to reduce the task's duration. However, there is a fundamental problem with 'crashing' – it frequently doesn't work.

Let's start with a simple example to explain that statement. You're cleaning a car. It looks like it's going to take up to an hour so you decide to 'crash' this task by adding more resources to get it back on track.

If two people clean the car then it looks like it will only take half an hour. However, if you keep adding people the task duration will not keep reducing forever. When there are six people around the car the cleaning will probably take slightly more than the 10 minutes you (mathematically) expect – one hour divided by six – because in real life, they'll be getting in each other's way. When the team is 10 then there are serious issues of who does what, and when you get to 100 then most of the team can't even get to the car!

The problem is equally true in projects as you add more people:

- The time to communicate and coordinate actions across the team increases as a percentage of the whole time for the given tasks.
- More people in the team means more interfaces between them and hence potential for misunderstanding.

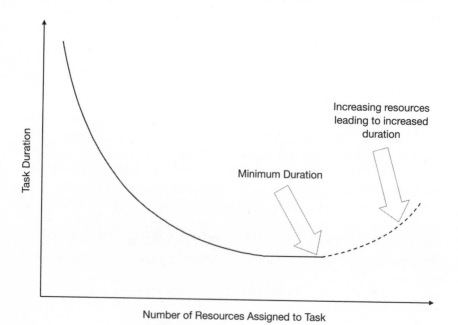

Figure 12.3 How increasing the number of people on a task can lead to increasing task durations

- 'New' people take time to understand what is involved in the task – draining time from both the management and the team.

This effect is shown in Figure 12.3.

To take account of this, the project manager can use a simple calculation for 'shared tasks' by **adding 10 per cent to the work content total for every extra person over six in the team working on that same task**. However, adding resources to a work package or task that is already in trouble will often make it even later!

This problem was most notably explained as 'Brooks Law' in 1975 by Fred Brooks in his book, *The Mythical Man Month*. His view was based on experience of issues being created at the interfaces between software programmers as the team is enlarged to catch up. Confusion, mis-communication and time wasted getting people up to speed can make things worse when resources are added to a task that is already in deep trouble.

Senior managers might not like the results but you have the evidence

Imagine you had a plan where you put someone down for 40 hours a week who was only really pushing things forward during 14 hours – how badly wrong would that be? How fast would you suddenly have uncontrollable delays and be in serious trouble?

Other people might not like the results but the question is can they disagree with them? If that is the person's real availability, you have to work with it. You have the evidence to back you up and so should be in a stronger position if you are lobbying for more resources or for a change in an individual's responsibilities.

Now we have the tasks, their work content and the resources assigned to them. The next step is to establish the exact relationships between them. The next chapter will describe the different types of 'dependencies' that define how different tasks can relate to one another.

Resource availability: summary and actions

1. For large teams of interchangeable personnel, you can use a blanket assumption:

    $$\text{Duration for task} = \frac{\text{Work content (days)}}{0.7 \text{ (availability)} \times \text{Full Time Equivalents committed}}$$

    This should be used carefully for very early estimates of duration and within large teams of identical, and essentially interchangeable, people working on the same tasks. Try to avoid any estimate becoming 'public' at this stage as it may be held against you later on.

2. The general assumption of 0.7 (70 per cent) availability relates to losing 10 per cent of working days to holidays and 20 per cent of work time to distractions, meetings, discussions, etc.

3. If there are more than six people working on the same task, add an extra 10 per cent to the work content for every person above six. This will allow for the increased complexity and extra communication needed when sharing a task.

4. The broad assumptions of availability are rarely true and, in particular for key people, you need to use their real availability, with dedicated calendars reflecting their actual availability to progress the project.

5. Talk to the team to explain the approach and get them to map out their regular commitments (meetings, training, client conferences) and detail other time lost to the project (holidays, etc).

6. Create a dedicated calendar for each person, reflecting their true availability to progress the project.

7. Ensure that the availability information is updated by asking project team members to report any changes, holidays planned, etc in their weekly project update given to the project manager.

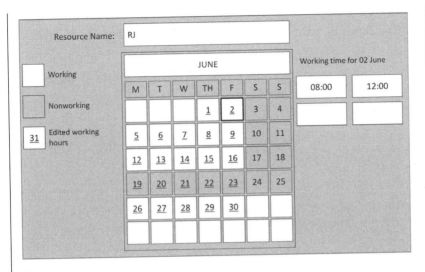

Figure 12.4 Example calendar for a resource with reduced availability

8. Assess the availability of other scarce resources in the project, eg test facilities or pilot plant. These should be managed in the same way as people in the project. This means there may need to be a calendar for the resources so that the software can calculate correct durations for tasks involving them.

13

Dependencies

 Dependencies show the relationships between different tasks.

You should now have developed and resourced tasks and understand the amount of work required to complete them. The next stage is to structure the tasks together to identify the dependencies between them, eg which tasks need to be completed before others start. It is only when you have this information that you can understand exactly how long the tasks should take. This is because the real availability of resources changes from week to week and so the exact duration of each task will depend on when the task kicks off.

Remember that some tasks have a natural dependency between them. You cannot, for example, walk in space before you've ridden the rocket up there. However, as project manager, you can also impose dependencies between tasks to force tasks to start or finish at the same time. There may not be a 'natural' reason for the relationship between the two (or more) tasks but it may be necessary or logical to put a dependency in place.

Rather than have to write that you 'do A, then B, C starts when B starts, D follows on from A', these dependencies can be created and shown graphically using project management software.

DIFFERENT TYPES OF DEPENDENCIES

These different examples will show the relationship between two tasks – A and B.

Finish-to-start (FS) dependencies

Task B can only start when task A has finished

Graphically this type of dependency would be as in Figure 13.1.

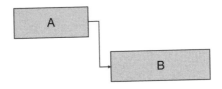

Figure 13.1 A finish-to-start dependency

This is the most common type of dependency you will find in projects. Examples of FS dependencies are:

- the roof cannot be put on a house until the walls are in place;
- engine testing cannot begin until the engine is assembled.

Start-to-start (SS) dependencies

B will start at the same time as A

There are not as many tasks that are like this, but defining certain tasks to start at the same time can be useful.

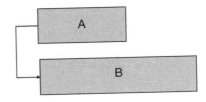

Figure 13.2 A start-to-start dependency

Examples of SS dependencies are:

- exams in university B start at the same time as in university A;
- extraction fans start when the oven heating cycle begins.

Finish-to-finish (FF) dependencies

Task B cannot finish until task A has finished

Finish-to-finish dependencies may seem unusual at first, but there are many tasks where one task can only be finished when a different task is complete. In this case, you can use FF constraints to show this relationship.

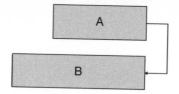

Figure 13.3 A finish-to-finish dependency

An example of an FF dependency is:

- reviewing the manual can only finish when writing the manual is complete;
- inspecting the car welding cannot finish until the welding is complete.

LAG

In the examples above, the dependencies were immediate, eg in the finish-to-start dependency, task B followed task A straight away. However, there are tasks which, although related, cannot happen immediately. You can't paint plaster until it's dry. You can't build walls until the foundations are set.

This means that you need to be able to introduce the concept of 'lag' between tasks. This is a delay that you can define between tasks once the dependency condition has been met (see Figure 13.4).

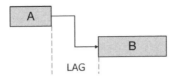

Figure 13.4 Lag in a finish-to-start dependency

For example, defining a five-day lag figure in a finish-to-start relationship means the second task will only start five days later (as shown in Figure 13.5).

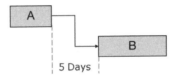

Figure 13.5 Five days lag in a finish-to-start dependency

The different types of dependencies with lag periods introduced would therefore look as shown in Figure 13.6.

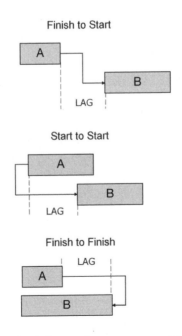

Figure 13.6 The standard dependency types with lag

PREDECESSORS AND SUCCESSORS

Any task can have multiple dependencies and these can be a mix of the different types, as shown in Figure 13.7.

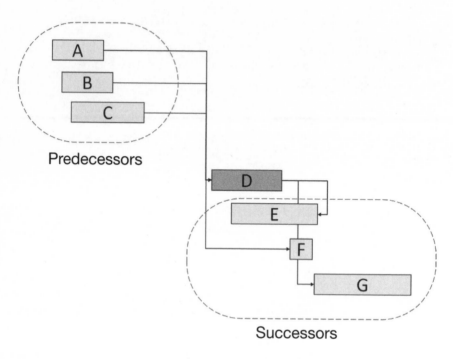

Figure 13.7 Example of different dependencies between tasks

The diagram shows the following relationships:

- Tasks A, B and C are called the predecessors to task D. Task D depends on them to start.
- Tasks E, F and G are called the successors of task D. They depend on task D to start.
- Task D has a finish-to-start relationship with A, B and C. In this case, all three predecessors must be finished before D can start.
- Task F has a lagging start-to-start relationship with D (F starts a set lag period after task D starts).
- Task G has a finish-to-start relationship with task D with lag (G will start after the lag period from the end of D).

- Task E has a finish-to-finish relationship with lag to task D and so cannot finish until after the lag period at the end of task D.

The relationships between different tasks can be clearly displayed in project management software where you can see:

- the predecessors and successors (the task numbers/letters);
- the type of dependency (FF, FS, SS);
- any lag value (normally shown as days but configurable in the software).

Task D from Figure 13.7 could be shown as follows (with values for lag, eg +5d means a 5 day log):

Task	D
Predecessors	1, 2, 3
Successors	E (FF + 5d), F (FS + 3d), G (SS + 7d)

In Microsoft Project, the same tasks and predecessor/successor information would look as it does in Figure 13.8.

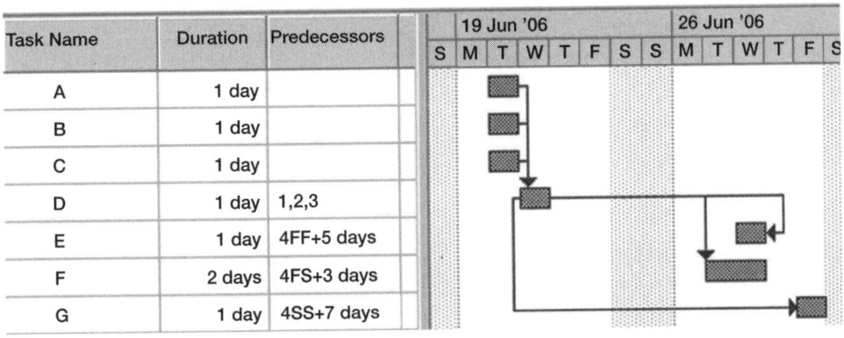

Figure 13.8 Gantt chart view of dependencies in Figure 13.7

TASKS AND SUB-TASKS

As discussed in Chapter 9 on work breakdown structure, tasks can be broken down into sub-tasks, as shown in Figure 13.9.

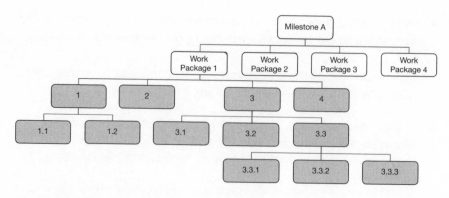

Figure 13.9 Example work breakdown structure

Figure 13.10 shows a Microsoft Project version of the same work breakdown with durations added.

	❶	Task Name	Duration	Start	WBS	Predecessors	19 Jun '06 / 26 Jun '06 / 03 J
1		⊟ Task 1	2 days	Tue 20/06/06	1		
2		Task 1.1	1 day	Tue 20/06/06	1.1		
3		Task 1.2	1 day	Wed 21/06/06	1.2	2	
4		Task 2	1 day	Thu 22/06/06	2	1	
5		⊟ Task 3	5 days	Fri 23/06/06	3	4	
6		Task 3.1	1 day	Fri 23/06/06	3.1		
7		Task 3.2	1 day	Mon 26/06/06	3.2	6	
8		⊟ Task 3.3	3 days	Tue 27/06/06	3.3	7	
9		Task 3.3.1	1 day	Tue 27/06/06	3.3.1		
10		Task 3.3.2	1 day	Wed 28/06/06	3.3.2	9	
11		Task 3.3.3	1 day	Thu 29/06/06	3.3.3	10	
12		Task 4	1 day	Fri 30/06/06	4	5	

Figure 13.10 Gantt chart view of the work breakdown structure shown in Figure 13.9

Tasks with sub-tasks are shown as a black bar and are called **'summary tasks'**.

For example, Task 1 has a black bar that is as long as the duration of the sub-tasks (1.1 and 1.2). In other words, Task 1 does not have a duration assigned to it by you – the software sets the duration of this summary task as being equal to the tasks underneath it.

Task 2 has no sub-tasks and so is shown as an ordinary task rather than a summary task.

The reason you need to get this clear is that sometimes people end up assigning resources to tasks and the sub-tasks underneath them – creating a doubling of assigned resources and some world-class head scratching. An example may clarify this effect.

Consider a project to build a house. You could produce a plan with only one task lasting one year and with 10 people working on it. This might be a reasonable estimate of the work needed to complete the house. However, the plan is a bit short on detail. So you create some sequential sub-tasks to complete the foundations, walls and roof.

For simplicity's sake, let's say each one lasts four months and needs 10 people to complete. You assign the resources to each one of the three sub-tasks. At this point the resourcing will be wrong because you assigned resources to a task (10 people building the house for a year) and also to the sub-tasks (10 people doing the foundations, the walls and then the roof). The resource usage will now show 20 people working on the house during the build.

If you cannot explain an over-assignment in a project plan then have a look at the usage of that particular resource. This will enable you to see if you have tripped over this problem as the list of tasks they are working on at any point would list both a summary task and one or more sub-tasks. You correct this problem by removing resources from any summary task.

Unlike resourcing tasks, it is fine to create dependencies at either the task or the sub-task level.

CRITICAL PATH

 The critical path is the set of activities that need to be finished on time for the project to be completed on schedule. The scheduled date is driven by this set of tasks.

Figure 13.11 shows various different groups of tasks leading through to a milestone (represented by a black diamond in most software packages).

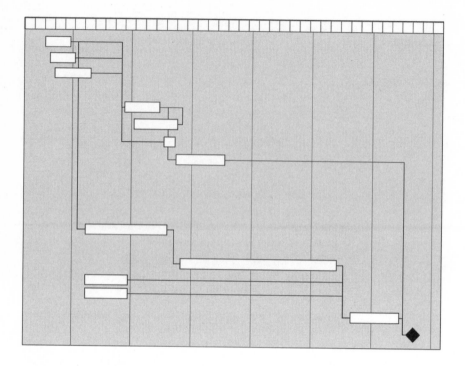

Figure 13.11 Example Gantt chart

Figure 13.12 shows the same information but with the tasks on the critical path shown as dark boxes.

The critical path is the longest duration path through the tasks in the plan.

A simple test to know if a task is on the critical path is to add a day to the duration of the task and see if the end date also changes. If it does then the task is indeed on the critical path and vice versa. Project management software can help you here by indicating the critical path for you automatically, but you need to understand the concept.

The tasks on the critical path are those you need to focus attention on as overruns here will have a direct effect on the duration of that part of the project. As the project proceeds, other tasks may overrun with the result that a different path through the tasks may become critical. When this happens, these should instantly become the tasks you are most focused on managing and, where necessary, de-risking. This will be discussed more in Chapter 15, 'Optimizing the Plan'.

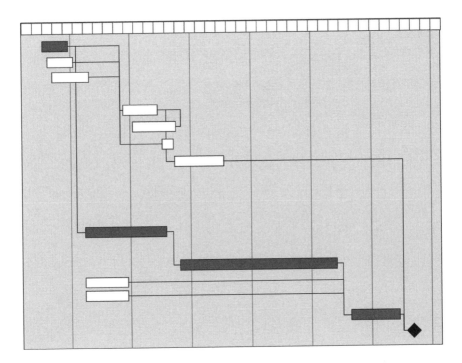

Figure 13.12 Gantt chart with critical path displayed

SLACK/FLOAT

In Figure 13.13, the set of tasks leading to task A forms the critical path. The other leg to B can be delayed without 'pushing' the end date of the project back in time.

 The amount of time that this leg of the project can slip without having an impact on the project is called slack or float.

Free slack is the amount of time a task can be delayed without delaying its successor.

Total slack is the amount of time a task can be delayed without delaying completion of the project.

In Figure 13.13, task A is on the critical path but task B can overrun a certain amount without it coming onto the critical path itself. The length of time that B can be delayed before this occurs is indicated as the float.

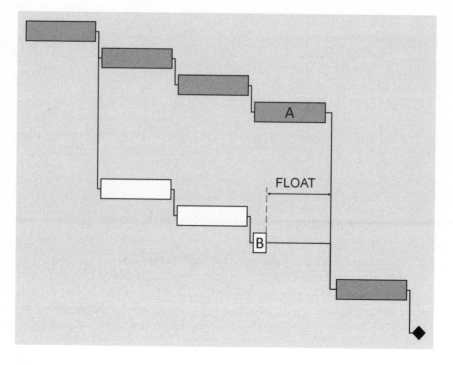

Figure 13.13 Float in a project plan

Dependencies: summary and actions

1. Dependencies show the relationships between a given task and the tasks that precede it (predecessors) and follow it (successors).
2. Dependencies include constraints that define the relationship between the predecessor and successor task(s):
   - finish-to-start – the successor cannot begin until the predecessor is complete;
   - start-to-start – the successor cannot begin until the predecessor has begun;
   - finish-to-finish – the successor cannot finish until the predecessor has finished.
3. Delays can be added to these constraints to create 'lag' in the plan – eg, the successor has to wait a given time after the end of the predecessor until it can begin.

4. The amount of time that this leg of the project can slip without having an impact on the project is called 'slack' or 'float'.

5. The critical path is the set of activities that need to be finished on time for the project to be completed on schedule. The scheduled date for completion of the project is driven by this set of tasks.

6. Work with the team to define the relationships between tasks created during the work. This can be done directly using project management software or on paper. Either approach works but it is the involvement of the project team that is most important:

   - identify which tasks are related to other tasks;
   - for each task, identify the type of dependency involved. Remember it is unlikely that there will be many 'start-to-start or 'finish-to-finish' dependencies – most will be 'finish-to-start';
   - establish if the successor task will begin immediately or if there will be any delay (lag) that will occur or needs to be put into the plan to reflect reality.

7. Enter there relationships into the task list in your project management software.

14

Risk and Mitigation

What you don't know can hurt you – and almost certainly will!

The work outlined in previous chapters will eliminate many risks that projects face due to confusion, lack of planning and poor estimation. However, many other things can and certainly will go wrong during the life of your project. This is why an 'everything goes right' plan never works, because there's no allowance for the problems and delays that occur.

As a project manager, you should be identifying risks within the project and determining which ones need to be managed and how.

 Risk management is the process of identifying and categorizing potential risks and then defining actions to mitigate these risks.

Contingency plans may be needed to provide a fall-back position if things go wrong.

'Contingency, contingency, contingency. You're going to contingency this project out of existence!'

So said the Programme Director of a major telecoms infrastructure project. I had to feel sorry for him as my team had identified some major problems with the project and needed to re-plan. He could only see his job being under pressure and although I'm sure he 'knew' that I was right, he couldn't bring himself to accept the truth, as he saw it as signing his career death warrant. He persisted with impossible dates and, pretty soon, the inability to adhere to those meant that he was taken off the project. Sometimes there is no right answer, but you can only bury your head in the sand for so long before reality will steamroller over you.

THE PROBLEMS WITH SIMPLE RISK/ CONTINGENCY PLANNING

The simplest way that risks are managed is by the introduction of 'contingency' time into the project. This adds extra time to tasks to allow for things to go wrong. For example, you might add a blanket figure of 15 per cent to every work content value in the project.

When you are taking a high-level look at the overall project, these blanket assumptions appear to make sense. They provide a buffer to the unforeseen problems that will occur. However, when you start to manage the project on a day-to-day basis you will have much better, and more specific, information about the upcoming elements in the plan. The general contingency allowance will now appear very crude because it is smoothed across the life of the project and takes no account of specific risks that you can clearly see at this point.

By applying a blanket contingency factor to a project, you are only doing one thing to mitigate the effect of problems in the plan – adding time.

IDENTIFYING AND MANAGING RISKS

There are classically a number of stages to developing contingency plans within a project:

1. Identify potential sources of risk.
2. Understand the probability of each risk and the effect on the project if it happens.
3. Consider the impact of all risks on the overall project.
4. Develop ways to avoid or mitigate (reduce the impact of) the risk.

The following sections will look at dealing with risks to the project in more detail.

RISK IDENTIFICATION

There are two types of risk that you deal with:

●   certain – those that will definitely occur at some point; and
●   uncertain – those that may occur at some point.

For some risks you will know when the risk will occur, while for others there is no way of predicting when it might happen. Figure 14.1 plots the different categories that risks can fall into.

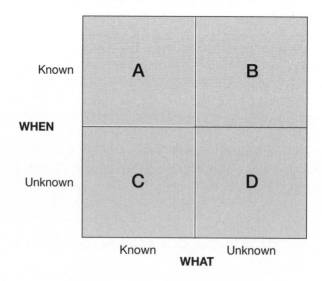

Figure 14.1 Types of risk

Examples of risks within each category are:

A: US electricity demand peaks during half-time of the Super Bowl.
B: Opening a new bridge. Starting up a nuclear reactor.
C: Earthquake in San Francisco.
D: Could be anything!

You can spot risks in the project at almost any time. You shouldn't just be thinking about risks during weekly meetings with the team – you should be looking for potential risks all of the time. You will trip over them during discussions with team members, reading status reports, attending site visits, analysing results, etc. The important thing is to make sure the risk is recorded so that it can then be assessed for its impact on the project.

If you don't record the risk, you can't share it with the rest of the team. It may be painful but it doesn't take long to do and your judgement might just be wrong – the risk you think is insignificant might actually be a complete showstopper.

As a practical point, you also want to be seen to be doing an efficient job of managing the project, so don't open yourself up to criticism by leaving risks apparently unmanaged.

RISK ASSESSMENT

Some risks are incredibly serious but exceptionally unlikely to happen. Some are the reverse, with a very high probability but only a low impact on the project. If you had infinite resources you might chase down every single risk, but you don't and you can't. The skill of a project manager is in juggling limited resources, and dealing with risk is no different. You will have to identify which risks you manage and which one's you can ignore.

One way to do this is to carry out an evaluation of each risk as it occurs during the project, and to record the characteristics of each against:

- **impact** – how severe it will be for the project if the risk happens;
- **probability** – what the likelihood is that the risk will happen.

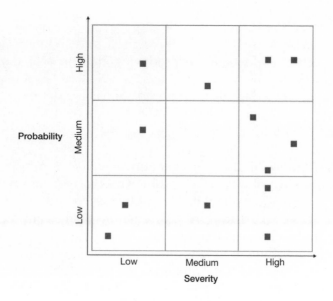

Figure 14.2 Example of probability and impact of project risks

You can map the project risks as shown in Figure 14.2. How would you deal with what you see in Figure 14.2?

Clearly the first priority must be the risks that are high in both severity and probability – they're likely to bite you and they'll bite you hard. That was an easy question; let's try something harder. Which risks do you deal with next?

To illustrate this, Figure 14.3 doesn't show the individual risks; instead the seriousness of each combination of risk and probability is displayed with darker blocks representing more serious risks.

To be very clear on this, I recommend that you deal with the risks in the order shown in Figure 14.4.

Note that I suggest dealing with high severity risk even if it is low probability (4) before the opposite case (5).

However, in this discussion of risk and probability there is an important element missing – time. How quickly should the risk be dealt with? To factor this third dimension in we need to create a composite score that combines the ratings for risk, probability and time.

Each risk is added to a 'risk register' (with any reference to external materials, files, photos, reports, etc). This document is regularly added to during the life of the project as new risks are identified.

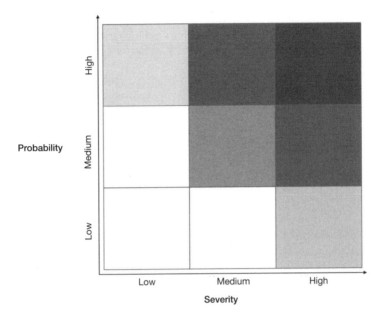

Figure 14.3 Severity of risks displayed against impact and probability

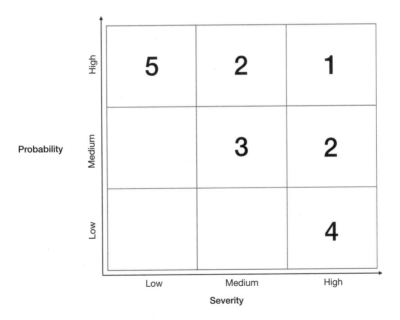

Figure 14.4 Order for tackling risks sorted by probability and impact

Rank	Problem Description	A Impact 1–5	B Probability 1–5	C Time Urgency 1–3	= A.B.C Score 1–75	Resp.	Actions
1	Failure to secure WiMAX mast site contract	4	5	3	48	HAJ	Seek second source of mast sites from international broker or local GSM companies
2	In building penetration below 'calculated' levels	5	4	2	40	KGS	Carry out field trials with three potential vendors in 'real world' conditions
3							
4							
5							

Figure 14.5 Example risk register

An example is shown in Figure 14.5, in which risk number 1 gets a score of 48.

The criteria for the 'time urgency' score will depend on the overall duration of the project. For example, in a shorter project you might set the scores for time urgency as follows:

1   for risks likely to happen later than **three months** from now;
2   for risks likely to happen later than **two months** from now;
3   for risks likely to happen later than **one month** from now.

In a longer project you might set different scores for time urgency:

1   for risks likely to happen later than **six months** from now;
2   for risks likely to happen later than **three months** from now;
3   for risks likely to happen later than **one month** from now.

The composite score for risk, probability and time can be used to compare different risks and decide which ones should be dealt with and in what priority. The project manager can then define the actions for each risk and assign resources to carry them out.

One quick word of advice here. The figures calculated in the risk assessment are designed to be a guide but do not mean you can turn your brain off. Consider the risks carefully and then select the actions you think are necessary. It's your neck on the line.

A telecom company was having difficulty planning the deployment of its new masts. The easy to access sites had been taken by the existing mobile phone operators and so the company would not always be successful with an application. The problem was that it was planning for success and could not model failure.

In reality, a successful application would take 13 months from start to the site being live, while an unsuccessful application would lead to a search for an alternative site. This would typically mean 21 months to get a site up and running.

Talking to the implementation team indicated that in 75 per cent of cases, the application would proceed without a hitch, 25 per cent of the time the application would fail and they would need to find an alternative site. This failure rate could actually be planned for, but the company stuck with the assumption that every site would work fine. The result is it went way over delivery schedule, a major slice of investment did not become available and the business failed spectacularly!

RISK REDUCTION

There are a number of ways of reducing risks in the project.

Avoidance

You can try to avoid the risk by changing the circumstances so that you don't encounter the risk; see Table 14.1.

Consider the risk you are facing in your own project and ask yourself (and the team), 'What could we do to avoid this risk completely?'

Contingency

If the risk cannot be avoided, you need to put in place contingency measures to reduce the potential impact. There are many ways you can do this, for example:

Table 14.1 Avoiding risks

Type of risk	What you do	Examples
Time-related risk	Change the timescales to avoid the risky period	Don't plan to build in a country during its hurricane season
		Don't plan the first sea trials of a ship in winter when the seas might be too rough
Company-related risk	Change the relationship or add suppliers/partners to remove issues	Major corporations like GM evaluate suppliers for the risk of insolvency or inability to respond to problems
		Chip companies like TI use more than one fabrication plant to reduce the risk of failure to supply

- Provide a parallel set of tasks that aim to achieve the same end result in a different way (meaning one of the two approaches might deliver the desired result even if the other fails) – eg a second development programme using a different technology.
- Apply more resources to a task or work package that is under threat of not delivering (this could be more hands to help out or it could be expertise).
- Carry out detailed planning to provide more accurate estimates. This will allow extra resources to be assigned, timescales changed, etc as necessary.
- Carry out a study to find ways to avoid the problem.
- Put more time into the project to allow for contingencies.
- Encourage suppliers by setting up contracts to penalize under-performance, lateness, etc.
- Take out insurance against certain risks occurring.

RISK MANAGEMENT

You need to make assessing risks part of weekly meetings with the project team. This may be relatively quick when there are no high-priority risks to deal with, but on other occasions you will have a very serious new risk to discuss and you'll need to give it time.

Don't worry if the discussion is taking a while. Part of the purpose of a weekly project meeting is to identify, evaluate and find resolutions to risks. Let the brain power in the room do its stuff while the team are still making progress. However, you should also recognize when the discussions are going round in circles or when there is an opportunity to deal with the problem offline in a smaller group.

Ensure that the risk list is updated and circulated before the weekly meeting so that people can consider newly identified risks and also correct any errors or omissions. The meeting should then go through the list of the most serious risks and consider progress on actions to date.

For new risks, the team should either carry out an assessment or consider the results of any assessment already completed. They should then identify possible actions to avoid completely, limit the impact or reduce the probability of occurrence of the risk.

Any updates or changes decided upon during the meeting should be integrated immediately into the risk list.

To help drill down into risks and get closer to potential solutions, some techniques for problem solving are included in Appendix 4.

At the extreme of technology risk – the F22 Raptor

The Raptor is an extraordinary aircraft. Designed to replace the F15, the Raptor entered development in 1986 and the prototypes first flew in 1992. The first production plane was delivered in 2003.

The plane is probably the most effective air superiority fighter in the world and possesses a combination of exceptional manoeuvrability, high speed (close to Mach 2) and stealth design/materials that make it near invisible to radar. To maintain the low radar profile, missiles are stored inside the aircraft until just before firing, when they are pushed out and launched in less than a second.

A 2004 report by the General Accounting Office (GAO) identified this project as combining significant risk with 'onerous technology challenges'. That probably understates some of the problems faced by Boeing and Lockheed – the two main contractors.

Though the aircraft is an amazing technical achievement, the technology risks faced have led to the significant delays and cost over-runs, shown in Table 14.2.

Table 14.2 Over-runs in the Raptor project

	1986 Estimates	Reality
R&D Spend	US $21 billion	US $31 billion (as of 01/2004)
Development Programme	9 years	19 years
Time to Production Delivery	9 years	19 years

Risk and mitigation: summary and actions

1. Identify and deal with risks as early as you can in the life of the project – it's less expensive.
2. Identify and record the potential risks in the risk list.
3. Evaluate each risk against probability, impact on the project and how soon the risk needs to be addressed.

Rank	Problem Description	A Impact 1–5	B Probability 1–5	C Time Urgency 1–3	= A.B.C Score 1–75	Resp.	Actions
1	Failure to secure WiMAX mast site contract	4	5	3	48	HAJ	Seek second source of mast sites from international broker or local GSM companies
2	In building penetration below 'calculated' levels	5	4	2	40	KGS	Carry out field trials with three potential vendors in 'real world' conditions
3							
4							
5							

Figure 14.6 Example risk register

4. Reduce the potential impact of the risks you have identified by:

    ● Avoiding risks: change when you will carry out certain tasks if there is a particular time window that creates the risk; change the relationship with suppliers/partners.
    ● Building in contingency:
        – start parallel work to deliver the same result as a risky part of the project but in a different way;
        – apply more resources;
        – carry out more planning to improve the accuracy of estimates (and hence respond to any problems identified);
        – add more time to the planned duration.

5. The risk list should be reviewed on a weekly basis and the status updated.

Part IV

Getting the Plan Right

15

Optimizing the Plan

The interesting thing is that what you have now looks like a project plan. You have worked from the project's objective and underlying milestones and have:

- everybody's accurate estimates;
- resourced the tasks carefully;
- ensured that no one is planned to do more than the amount of work they are available to do;
- created a structured project plan.

The only difficulty now is that the end date will be much later than you expected!

The good news is that this is normal at this point. However, before you relax too much, I should warn you that it's about to get worse.

Remember that the resources and the tasks can be put in place in a variety of different ways and it is a bit like trying to pack a suitcase. There are different ways to do this and some will be better than others. It's time for some reorganization to get the best result possible for the project as it stands.

There are a few places we need to start looking to figure out how to take time out of the project if that is the problem (and it normally is at this stage).

CREATE MORE REALISTIC RESOURCE USAGE

You have selected resources to do particular tasks but these choices are unlikely to be the optimum choice for the project.

Levelling the plan

The first thing to do is to level the project plan. This is a feature in the software that will delay tasks where a resource is trying to do two (or more) things at once. These tasks might look fine drawn in parallel in the plan, but when you realize that a given resource is actually down to do 48 hours work on a given day, and is only available for three hours, then you know the plan is completely unrealistic.

Levelling eliminates this type of error by assigning the task durations (based on work content, of course) to the real availability of the resources. This ensures:

- no resource works more hours than it has available for the project on that day;
- tasks are spread over time and/or delayed until their use of resources is realistic;
- the number of resources defined as available in the project plan are used effectively (in other words levelling stops the plan assuming you have more resources available than is true).

Levelling is best done by software as it can become very complicated and you will need to come back to it several times as you optimize the plan. However, it is never done perfectly and you tend to find levelling produces huge holes in the plan that you will need to remove by applying your brain to the problem.

You will notice also that the project duration is now even longer than it was before (I said it was going to get worse before it gets better).

IMPROVE RESOURCE USAGE TO SHORTEN THE DURATION OF KEY TASKS

The critical path is the set of tasks that are driving the end date of the project. To finish the project more quickly you must therefore shorten this set of tasks. Once you have identified the critical path, you can start to shorten the duration of the individual tasks that lie on the path.

Remove holes from the critical path

If the critical path looks like the one in Figure 15.1, there is a gap between tasks that needs to be explained and potentially removed. I say 'potentially' because it's possible the project timescales are actually fine. However, it is almost certain that the current project plan is too long and needs to be shortened.

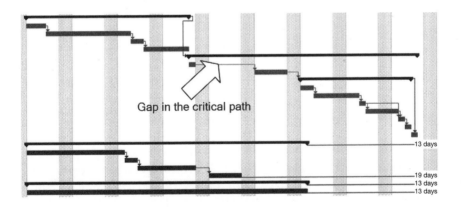

Figure 15.1 Gantt chart showing a gap in the critical path

Any gaps between tasks on the critical path could be there due to:

- a dependency condition (such as a lag between the finish of one task and the beginning of the next);
- the unavailability of a resource required by the critical path task following the gap.

If the gap is because of a dependency condition you need to consider:

- if any lag imposed between the tasks is realistic and if there are any ways to remove it.
  - If it is something drying, can you dry it faster? Can you change the material to one that dries faster?
  - If you will be waiting for testing by the quality department, could the product be fast-tracked? Could an external company do it faster?
  - whether some form of date constraint has been imposed on the task following the gap, eg the task must start on, or cannot start before, a given date. If this is the case then is this constraint realistic and can you change the situation so that the constraint becomes unnecessary?

If there is no lag condition or constraint delaying the task, you need to look at the resources used in the delayed task. The likelihood is that the levelling of the project will have put one (or more) of the resources on a less important task, meaning that the task on the critical path has to wait for this resource to become available, as shown in Figure 15.2.

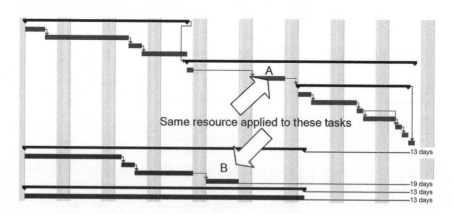

Figure 15.2 Gantt chart showing resource applied incorrectly

In the example in the figure, a resource is working full time on task B, which is not on the critical path, rather than task A, which is. This will delay the end of the project.

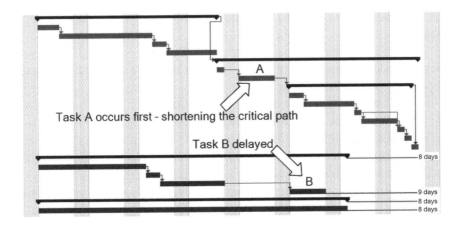

Figure 15.3 Gantt chart showing the resourcing problem fixed and the critical path gap removed

To shorten the project duration, task A should be done first, or at worst at the same time as B. This means you either need to ensure the resource carries out task A first or that a different resource is used to avoid the clash of timescales. The modified Gantt chart for this example would look like Figure 15.3.

To identify resources that are important on the critical path, it is necessary to understand more about the way project management software works. Normally these packages have some sort of resource usage view that allows you to see:

- how many of a particular type of resource are available;
- what each is doing on a given day/week;
- what they are working on currently.

If you go to the resource part of the software package, you will see that you can define the number of particular resources you have available to you. Without cloning people we can't actually increase the number of key individuals on the project, but we can use the software to identify where they are constraining the project.

The software doesn't know the difference between a unique individual (a person) and an injection moulding machine. It doesn't know when the project has access to one of a given resource or 200 – you have to tell it. You do this by setting a maximum number of each type of resource involved in the project – eg one laser oblation unit, three dicing machines, one Richard Jones, one Mark Watt, etc.

Project management software is designed to allow you to change the number of resources either to reflect the real situation in your business or to play out some 'what if' scenarios and see what the effect of changing resources would be. This is exactly what we are going to do to identify which resources are causing problems on the critical path.

The approach to use is to change the available number for a given resource and look for changes to the end date of the project. In other words, change the number of resources called Jessica Mason from one to two. The software doesn't know this is impossible and will recalculate the duration of all of Jessica's tasks as if there were two of her.

For most resources this type of change will have little impact on the end date and so they are not of interest in this part of the optimization. However, if the end date of the project changes dramatically as you change the number of a particular resource, then you have identified at least one 'critical resource'.

Note: remember to put these resource numbers back to their previous values unless you have spare resources of this type and want to make the change permanent.

The next step to shorten the overall duration of the project is to look at the critical path tasks where the critical resource is used and swap the critical resource for a different team member. If the end date does not move then it is clear you have fixed a problem with part of the plan that is not on the critical path. Replacing the critical resource in their tasks in this part of the project is very unlikely to improve the duration – it is their use on the critical path that is causing the problem.

As we make a change there may well be a negative impact on another part of the project and so you should keep referring back to the critical path to ensure you have not introduced a new gap, to check how the end date is looking and to make sure that another part of the project has not switched to become the new critical path.

It is common sense that you should look to replace heavily used resources with the most lightly used ones where they have similarly appropriate skills and capabilities. This will minimize the likelihood of knock-on effects with the plan where you solve one resource constraint problem but create another.

When you are considering using a subcontractor to substitute for a critical resource, you should also consider the extra management time needed to manage this external relationship. The time, and sometimes stress, are not insignificant and your preference should be to use 'internal' resources where you can.

REDUCING TASK DURATIONS ON THE CRITICAL PATH

If the project is still predicted to end 'too late' in relation to the objectives, the next stage is to shorten the durations of tasks on the critical path. This is done by adding resources to each task and seeing how this impacts the overall project duration.

Again, the resource numbers can be increased resource by resource to look at which changes have a significant impact on the overall duration. You may find that you have to go back and renegotiate with resource managers at this point. If you identify resources that can reduce the duration, assign them and look at the impact on the plan.

You may find that:

- optimizing one set of tasks delays other so that the project would take even longer;
- the original critical path changes after some optimization and another part of the project goes critical.

Neither of these is a major problem. Remember this is an iterative process. You make changes, see what the impact of those changes is, and undo them if you don't like the result.

WORKING IN PARALLEL

At this point, you have optimized the critical path from a resource perspective. The next stage is to look hard at the logic of what is happening. Time and again I see assumptions in projects that are not valid and that can be changed for the better with a bit of effort and pushing.

One key area is to look at what is currently sequential and to consider what could be done in parallel.

A company that makes plastic injection moulded components for inhalers was planning a series of new tools to progressively build up to full production of a new product.

Each moulded tool has a number of cavities and the company was planning to go through a single-cavity tool and then on to four- and finally 16-cavity tools. Each tool would require a full test cycle and the 16-cavity tools would create a great deal of complexity, as examples from each cavity were tested in combination with each other. The result was that the testing load would increase and the costs of tooling meant that the evolution from single- to four- to 16-cavity tooling would take considerable time.

At the end of this process was a very lengthy series of tasks to gain approval for the product from the regulatory authorities. The simple question that removed nearly nine months from the project was, 'Why wait to submit the 16-cavity product for approval – why not kick-off the process from the four-cavity tooling?'

No one could think of any good reason why this would be a problem. This allowed the 16-cavity tool development and the approval process to be carried out in parallel (concurrently) as opposed to the original plan, which was almost completely sequential.

OPTIMIZATION AND RISK

Look at Figure 15.4, which shows a project with 10 major elements that are predominantly in parallel. The duration of one is significantly longer than any other. If I want to reduce the overall project duration, I know exactly where I need to focus my attention. Problems in the first nine tasks may not cause any risk to completing the project on time, so I can focus management attention on the 10th task.

Optimization will reduce the duration of the project, but if you optimize the longest part of the project, you may find that another part of the project becomes close to the duration of the critical path.

After the optimization in Figure 15.5, it won't take much for task 3 to start pushing the project duration back. Instead of task 10 being the sole risk, there are now two tasks (10 and 3) that are risks to the overall project duration (and task 6 is not too far behind).

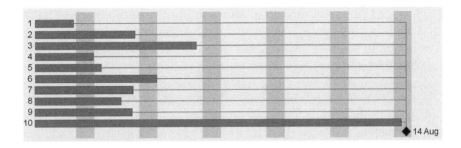

Figure 15.4 Parallel tasks with one clearly driving the completion date

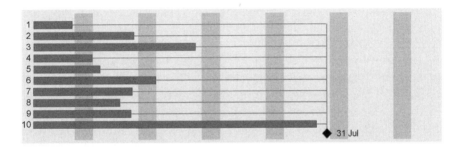

Figure 15.5 Shortened project duration with more tasks threatening to become the critical path

In the extreme case, all 10 tasks could end up having very similar durations and therefore problems with any one of them could delay the project.

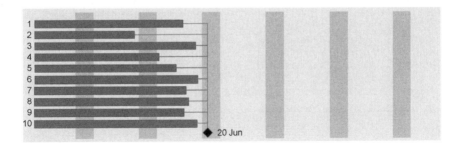

Figure 15.6 Shortest project duration but much higher risk of end date slipping

In the example in Figure 15.6, and sometimes in real projects, the trade-off for reducing the project duration is that the risk increases dramatically as more tasks could delay the overall project. The risk multiplied 10-fold in this case!

This situation creates headaches for project managers and team leaders as they are uncertain about where they need to focus their attention to manage risk effectively. The lesson is that, although we are reducing the timescales in the project, we are also increasing risk, and this needs to be reflected in the contingency applied to the project.

PROJECT CRASHING

At this point you are still trying to find the optimum version of the project that uses resources effectively. If the overall project or part of it is still too long, you may need to 'crash' the project by adding in more resources or considering an alternative approach. Project crashing allows the project manager to develop alternatives and costs for different changes to the project. The trade-offs between time saved and the costs incurred can then be debated and a decision made that fits the needs of the project.

Project crashing goes beyond the simple resource changes discussed earlier in this chapter, as the project manager might be suggesting radical changes to the project, eg outsourcing part of the project or cancelling a separate project to free-up resources.

You start by identifying the alternative ways that you can reduce the duration. This will probably involve considering several different parts of the current phase or overall project. For each potential change you need to quantify costs before and after the proposed change. In other words, what it will cost for that particular part of the project without any changes and what it will cost with the new approach to shortening the duration.

Let's look at an example where there are five different ways to reduce time in the project (A – E). The overall cost and duration of the project will change depending on which approach you choose.

This is where you need to construct a crash table to compare the cost against the benefit of the different options. In each case, the original and crashed durations and costs are entered. This allows you to calculate the weeks saved and the additional cost that would be incurred for each option.

By dividing the cost by the number of weeks saved you derive the cost to the project for each week saved by the different crash options, as shown in the right-hand column in Table 15.1.

Table 15.1 Savings from different crash options

Crash Ref	Duration			Cost (£000s)			Cost/ week saved
	Planned	Crash	Weeks Saved	Planned	Crash	Incremental Cost	
A	12	6	6	130	140	10	1.67
B	8	4	4	65	90	25	6.25
C	7	4	3	80	110	30	10
D	9	6	3	100	130	30	10
E	6	4	2	80	120	40	20

If we wanted to reduce the duration rationally, Figure 15.7 shows that we would choose option A, then B and so on until the duration was acceptable. Option A provides more 'bang per buck' in terms of time saved per pound spent compared to the others, and likewise B is apparently better value than C, D or E. Option A provides the lowest cost per week saved, so you would choose this option first.

The only exception to this rule might be if the crash table looked like Table 15.2. In this table, option A is still the most effective in terms of money spent to save a week of duration in the project. However, it is very expensive and represents a major reduction in timescales. If you really need to take 12 weeks out of the plan, then choose option A. However, if the four weeks saved by option B is sufficient to meet the required deadline for the project, implementing B is £32,000 less expensive overall compared to choosing option A.

Project crashing is a case of applying common sense to the situation and asking yourself questions such as, how much time does the project need to be reduced by?

If earlier completion of the project has no financial impact on the company then the extra cost has no corresponding benefit to justify it. If finishing early means a product gets to market 12 weeks earlier

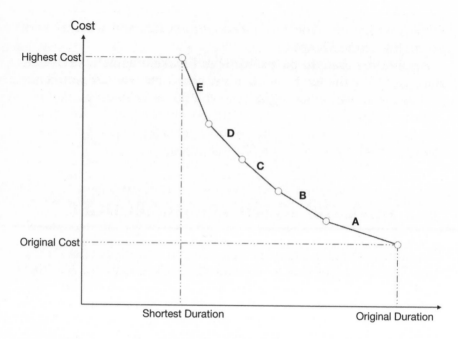

Figure 15.7 Cost and time saving of different project crash options

Table 15.2 Crash table options

| Crash ref | Duration | | | Cost (£000s) | | | |
	Planned	Crash	Weeks saved	Planned	Crash	Incremental cost	Cost/ week saved
A	24	12	12	150	200	50	4.17
B	8	4	4	32	50	18	4.50
C	7	4	3	40	55	15	5
D	9	7	2	60	70	10	5
E	6	5	1	60	70	10	10

(the difference between the time saving of A and B) then that has a value to the company. Go and talk to sales and marketing to see if they will be ready to launch the product earlier. If it can be launched earlier, is the extra cost of option A justified compared to the sales benefit to the company? Also ask yourself whether you need the extra time saving of option A as a contingency and whether it is worth the extra £32,000.

Apply your brain to the problem and make pragmatic decisions once you have the full facts. Involve the people who are recipients of the project in these decisions, whether it is sales/marketing, customers, engineering, manufacturing or whoever. If you don't, you might make the wrong decision, or get kicked even if you make the right one!

DEVELOPING THE PROJECT BUDGET

You now have the information necessary to create a budget for the project. The budget should include the work you have identified through the rolling wave planning, including costs for any risk management actions that are being taken or that are foreseen, and a reserve added to allow for uncertainties in the remaining phases of the project. The exact amount of reserve budget is hard to define as it varies from industry to industry, but can be as high as 50 per cent of the baseline budget at the start of software projects, for example.

Remember that you are managing risks **actively**, so some of the potential for overspend due to unforeseen issues is being managed out of the project. This should be reflected in lower reserve percentages than in projects that have poor risk management.

WHERE YOU END UP IS WHERE YOU START

So you have iterated around the same loop – looking at the resources for the task and amending resources until things improved. At a certain stage the project duration has been minimized or you have reached an appropriate trade-off between specification, quality, resources and timescales.

Sometimes this process will not lead to a plan that can meet the project's objectives. This allows you to signal this fact to senior management, customers or whoever. Having the evidence to back this up may actually 'free up' resources as senior managers loosen previously tight purse strings or make the 'impossible' decision they refused to make before. If not, then you're starting off in a bad place and no amount of platitudes about working hard are going to help you. Maybe it's time for you to write your CV, or you're going to have to pray that the gods of Project Management (I imagine them with lots of pens in their breast pockets) will smile on you and cut you some slack somewhere along the line.

This is the end of the creation of a realistic, resourced, objective-focused plan that the team has produced together. However, it is only the beginning of the project and the plan will begin to change almost immediately as things within the project evolve. The next part of this book describes how you keep up to date and how you recognize and resolve issues early before they become crises.

Part V

Staying on Track

16

Roles, Responsibilities and Communication

Let's start this chapter by looking at the different roles in the project. The following information will help you identify who does what.

PROJECT MANAGER

> Your job as a manager is to help your team do the work. Your success will come from providing them with what they need to succeed. (Jack Welch)

The project manager is the centre of the project, trying to juggle the different resources to deliver the project in the face of any challenges and changes. The project manager is responsible for:

- Assigning work directly to the project team members or to work package managers.
- Maintaining the top level plans by:

- ensuring the team is providing regular progress updates;
- integrating updates from the team at the work package and task level as appropriate.
- Taking a global view on the project to:
  - solve problems as they arise;
  - ensure risks are identified and managed within the team.
- Negotiating with resource managers (people, funding, equipment, facilities) to secure resources for the project.
- Providing updated and sufficiently detailed project plans and responsibilities to the team.
- Providing regular management reports summaries:
  - progress against the milestone plan;
  - costs versus budget (actual and predicted to end of project);
  - significant risks and mitigating actions;
  - potential 'show stopping' problems;
  - progress against gates (where the company has a 'stage-gate' process).
- Providing feedback on team members' performance for their evaluations.
- Maintaining the motivation and belief within the team.
- Keeping the project sponsor involved, informed and hopefully supportive of the project.

It is also important to keep perspective about the project.

Take time to take stock of where you are. Lots of good decisions can sometimes lead you to a bad place. In projects (and cars), you make the best decisions you can at the time but you can end up lost. If you keep your face in the spaghetti of project tasks and are running flat out, you are unlikely to spot that there is a quicker way to reach your destination.

Perhaps the most challenging problem you will face with your team will be where there is conflict. I can only pass on the following, based on bitter and occasionally bloody experience.

No one is worth keeping in the team 'at any price'.

When you have someone who is crucial to the project but is damaging to the team, you should try to limit the negative impact and also help them become more aware of the effect they have on others. Ultimately though, if that does not work, you need to take the hit and remove them from the project.

WORK PACKAGE OR MODULE MANAGERS

In larger projects you will not have direct control of all of the team. This may be because you are dealing with an outsourced part of the project or because there is someone managing this work. These people need to:

- Update their part of the project plan following the same principles as the overall plan (frequency, information used, etc).
- Provide key dates and progress information to the overall project manager.
- Identify and communicate new milestones and dependencies (particularly to other work packages) to the project manager as and when they occur.
- Ensure their team understand and execute tasks assigned to them.
- Identify risks and mitigate these where possible – communicating information about the risks and actions to the project manager.

PROJECT TEAM MEMBERS

Project team members are responsible for the execution of the tasks assigned to them but also contribute to the quality of planning and management of the project by:

- Finding gaps (missed tasks) or errors in the plan and communicating these up to the project or work package manager.
- Identifying risks to the timely success of the project.
- Regularly updating the work content remaining for ongoing tasks.

- Ensuring the plan reflects what is happening and communicating any variances to the project manager.
- Informing the project manager of their ongoing availability for the project.

The project plan may be updated by the project manager, but it is important to explain that it is every team member's responsibility to ensure the plan is accurate and up to date. It is vital that everyone believes and understands the plan and that action is taken to close any gaps between the plan, reality and belief within the team. It is extraordinarily damaging when team members think a project has become impossible but are not telling anyone.

As project manager it is your job to ensure the project and the team both start from the right place (a good, realistic, resourced plan) and stay there over the life of the project with regular updates.

PROJECT SPONSOR

Whether there is a project sponsor will vary from project to project according to the size of the project. The sponsor:

- Ensures the project is viable throughout its life in terms of:
  - business case;
  - delivery against objectives.
- Signs off the project definition document/charter.
- Resolves issues that may be beyond the authority or control of the project manager, eg:
  - negotiating with senior management and/or customers when there are major changes to the project specification;
  - obtaining increased financial, human or technical resources.
- Acts as chairman of the project steering group (sometimes called the 'project board'), if there is one.
- Signs off closure of the project when the project:
  - is stopped at a gate review;
  - cannot meet its next milestone;
  - is cancelled for other reasons;
  - has been completed (which is the desired outcome, of course).

PROJECT OFFICE

The project office is sometimes referred to as the 'project police' (or worse). It refers to a team of people who are tasked with maintaining the information and plan within the project. They have responsibility for the quality of the information but no formal authority in the plan. This can lead to issues with members of the project team who do not necessarily respect members of the project office and view their work as a bureaucratic overhead.

My approach to this is to view the project office team as full and equal members of the overall project team. They are incredibly valuable in providing the information that supports decision making and, although they are not moving the project forward directly, they are certainly helping keep it on track.

You need to impress on the project team that the project office is there to help them. Likewise, you need to ensure the project office is acting in a way that is consistent with your approach to project management. Some people in the project office may be very experienced and can provide valuable feedback and ideas on keeping the project on target.

The project needs to be managed your way, so you may also need to educate the members of the project office. You cannot have someone else's approach confusing the team or undermining what you are doing.

STEERING GROUP

A project steering group (sometimes called the 'project board' or 'project committee') is frequently used in larger projects to help maintain the direction of the project whilst ensuring input from relevant parties including customers, finance, marketing, customer support, engineering, etc.

Normally, the steering group is chaired by the project sponsor.

COMMUNICATION BETWEEN THE ROLES

There is no substitute for going around and talking to the team.

You have seen the roles of the different members of the expanded project team – now let's consider how you coordinate information between them.

Weekly meetings

These meetings provide opportunities to address new risks, reassign tasks, review progress, address issues and generally ensure that the project is on track.

The danger with these meetings is that they can be a very poor use of time for some team members. They may only need to provide input in one area of the project but have to sit through several hours of discussions that are irrelevant to them.

To reduce this problem, look carefully at the attendee list and if you can just call some people in when necessary, then do so instead of having them there for all of the meeting. They will probably be happier and can use the time saved to progress the project. However, if they want to attend the full meeting to keep on top of the overall project, let them.

The normal rules for success apply in these meetings:

- Ensure relevant information is circulated at least one day before the meeting to allow people time to read it and consider the contents.
- Have an agenda and, in advance, ask the team for any items they want added.
- Try to stick to time. I say 'try' because sometimes it really is important to have a successful meeting even if it's not one that runs to time. When you start, the best way to keep control of timing is to budget part of the meeting to each agenda item and try to stick to it.

- Ask someone to take notes during the meeting so you can concentrate on keeping things on track and listening to what is being discussed.

Team meetings are also a good time to check out how your team members are doing. Is anybody looking particularly tired? Are there tensions in the team? Is anyone over-stressed? As project manager you have a moral (not to mention a legal) duty to take care of the team. Yes, you want them to work hard and deliver, but unless you are trying to manage 100,000 slaves building a modern pyramid, you really don't want to have any casualties along the way.

Daily briefings

Daily briefings should be considerably shorter (say, 20 minutes) and be followed up by smaller group discussions if necessary.

One way to stop these carrying on for too long is to make them 'standing up' only. If people can't sit down (unless their health demands) then they tend to limit the off-topic stuff and keep things brief.

I recommend having briefings at the start of the day at the same time – eg 9 am. This makes them a regular fixture and everyone remembers what time they are held.

In larger teams, you can hold a briefing with team leaders, work package managers, etc and then they can hold a briefing within their own teams directly afterwards. I have found this approach (see Figure 16.1) very effective at ensuring good communication within the team without losing too much time doing it.

Phone conferences

Phone conferences serve a purpose but are less effective than meetings and can be more tiring. Listening to a crackly phone line and trying to understand what the mumbling person sitting a long way from the phone is saying can be really wearing.

The main reason I try to minimize the use of these is that you lose a lot in the communication by not being able to see the people involved. Without the body language it is harder to judge when

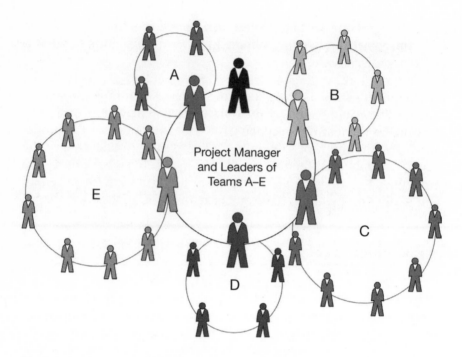

Figure 16.1 How information can be shared by team leaders across the wider project team

people are less comfortable and therefore when you should perhaps pay more attention.

Phone conferences are OK for day-to-day management of the project but are less suitable when there are major stresses or problems. If you have contentious issues to deal with, I would recommend handling them face-to-face where possible.

Video-conferencing

Projects involving a number of companies or different parts of an organization may need to use video-conferencing as a pragmatic way of holding meetings without losing huge amounts of time travelling.

Perception can be everything

On a multi-company project, I was asked to sort out one company (of the five) and then was asked to do the same sort of job on another company. These two main players were a five-hour drive apart and so I held video-conferences regularly.

When I sat at one end of these conferences I remember not having a clue why the other party were being so intransigent about some simple project-related issues. Later on when I sat at the other end of the conference call I remember the same thought occurring in the other direction.

The project's failings were driving a wedge between the teams and the video-conference was not helping to resolve them.

I believe teams should meet face-to-face where possible. However, if this is not feasible, you should try to ensure excellent communication and very good organization, and resolve contentious problems one-to-one where possible. Video-conferences are not the place for a fractious pair of teams to try to resolve serious differences.

PROJECT MANAGER'S WEEKLY CHECKLIST

Table 16.1 contains a reminder of the things that you should be doing (or considering) each week.

Table 16.1 Project manager's weekly checklist

Is the plan up to date?	Ensure you have feedback from individuals/teams working on elements of the project. This should be given to you on time and in the format you need.
Is the plan still realistic?	Take some time to think about whether the plan still represents what you are doing and what you should be doing!
Update the project status	The project may be part of a larger programme of activities; do you need to provide a weekly summary?
Are new risks being handled correctly?	Are new risks being identified and escalated by the project team? Have they been captured in the risk list and assessed for their seriousness within the project?
Have team members had up-to-date feedback on progress of the project?	Tell them about milestones passed, progress against targets, major changes, feedback from the project sponsor, customers, steering group, etc.
Do the project team know what to do?	Are they aware of the tasks they should be working on? Have they been told clearly about any changes in task priorities or objectives?
Is the team happy?	If everyone's happy you probably need to wake up and get to work because it's bound to be a dream. Human nature means there will always be some level of tension and unhappiness within a project. You need to look for, and resolve: • Serious tensions within the team; • Individuals who are over-stressed; • Individuals who are working too hard and/or risking burn out. Remember – your team's well-being is *your* responsibility.

Are regular team review meetings happening?	Are you keeping the team (or team leaders in larger projects) up to date with progress and allowing them to raise issues? Are team leaders and people managing work packages keeping their respective teams informed?
Have you got the right team?	Does the team have the right set of skills for the project? Have any gaps appeared? Is anyone not able to pull their weight? Who needs support in some way (help, training, praise)?
Is the team learning?	Are mistakes being repeated? Are new practices and approaches being shared across the team? Are new team members getting up to speed on the project quickly enough? If not, what can be changed to enable them to contribute more quickly?
Are you being consistent?	Remember consistency is vital to your credibility with the team. Are you keeping your promises and commitments?

17

Updating the Plan

The following is a very simple approach to updating a project plan. It applies the 'how far to go' principles for estimating work but requires only a small amount of time for project team members to complete whilst focusing your attention where it is needed.

THE UPDATE INFORMATION YOU NEED FROM TEAM MEMBERS

Team members working on active tasks should provide their best estimate of:

- How much work content remains to complete the task.
- How much work content they have managed to put into the task in the previous update period (normally a week).
- Whether the task has been completed, is still ongoing or is in trouble for some reason (with some supporting comments).

Figure 17.1 shows the format for a simple update form.

Project Name:		Work Content on Task (Days		Report By	
				Date	
Task Ref	Task Name	Achieved during period	Remaining	Status C = Completed O = Ongoing T = Trouble	Comments
1.1	Developing morping algorithm for multi-screen display	1.0	18	O	No current issues
2.6	Investigating power bug	2.5	?	T	Hit a brick wall and unsure how to proceed
2.7	Investigating alternative database access strategies	2.5	0	C	Completed to specification

Figure 17.1 Sample update information form

The reasons for asking for most of this information should be pretty clear by now. By asking for the work content remaining, you ensure the team member is focused on how far there is to go to get to the end of the task, rather than looking 'backwards' at out of date estimates.

INTEGRATING THE UPDATES

Just before the project kicks off, or before you begin to manage it with the new plan, you will have a fresh set of work content estimates. Over time this information will be updated, but this is the place where the original estimate can be a useful indicator.

Monitoring work content completed and remaining

Imagine the initial estimate for a task is 15 days of work content by a resource. From that point, you are asking the person carrying it out to report the work content remaining and the work content completed on the task during the week.

Let's be clear. The work content completed on the task is not the elapsed time someone has spent on it. It is the amount of time that the task has *really* been progressed during the week – ignoring holidays, training, interruptions, coffee breaks, etc – in other words, how much focused time the person has been able to spend progressing the task.

Let's consider the following example, which illustrates how this approach works.

Week 1

The people assigned to the task report back that they have done three days work content on the task and believe there are now seven days left. I've put this information into a table for clarity; see Table 17.1.

Table 17.1 Monitoring work completed and remaining – week 1

Task	A Original estimate (days)	Delta (B + C – A)	B Work content remaining	C Total work content to date	Week 1	Week 2	Week 3
Example	10	0	7	3	3		

The 'Delta' value is currently zero – in other words, they expected 10 days of work content and, with three done and seven left, there is no significant change in that situation.

In the second week, two days of work content are recorded with six days left. The latest estimate for work content remaining goes in column B and the running total of all the work content time carrying out the task goes in column C.

Table 17.2 Week 2

Task	A Original estimate (days)	Delta (B + C – A)	B Work content remaining	C Total work content to date	Week 1	Week 2	Week 3
Example	10	+1	6	5	3	2	

The delta value is now +1. This is still low so there's no particular need to worry.

In week 3, a further three days of work content are completed but the estimate for work content remaining has shot up to 10 days. This gives a delta figure of +8! Time to go and talk to these people and find out what's going on.

Table 17.3 Week 3

Task	A Original estimate (days)	Delta (B + C – A)	B Work content remaining	C Total work content to date	Week 1	Week 2	Week 3
Example	10	+8	10	8	3	2	3

This is not the same as using 'percentage complete'

At this point you could be wondering why I talked about the problems of percentage complete and yet am using the original estimates here. However, there is a clear difference.

The only values transferred into the plan are the work content remaining figures. The analysis described above is simply used to identify tasks where something significant has changed and help the project manager intervene to get to the bottom of things. It's an early warning system and not a planning tool.

UPDATING THE PLAN IN PRACTICE

The project plan will contain a list of tasks. This list can be cut and pasted into Excel to allow you to do the work content-based analysis described in Chapter 11.

You enter the estimates of work content remaining into this Excel spreadsheet. The list of tasks is identical in the project management software and Excel (you copied them, remember) and so you can copy the column of estimates of work content remaining back into the project management application. You effectively get two uses of the information but only type it in once. The only thing to be careful of is that your task list will be modified over time and Excel must reflect these changes to ensure the information is copied into the right places.

In the project management software, the estimates of work content remaining will be pasted over the estimates you had last week. If the figure for a particular task is zero, the task is treated as finished. Otherwise, the software will look at the availability of the resources assigned to tasks, combining this with the work content remaining to re-calculate the duration of each task. The dependencies between the tasks mean the software will instantly update the overall project duration and critical path.

You then need to look at the plan and consider how any changes need to be dealt with:

- Is the project still on time?
- Do you now need to optimize a different critical path?
- Is there a different branch of the project that is close to the same duration as the critical path? If so, how should this be treated?

HOW OFTEN?

The project plan should be updated weekly unless there are good reasons for doing otherwise. Establishing a routine and rhythm for updating is very useful as it helps the team adapt to this style of management and deliver what is required in terms of information.

Keep your project summary information up to date. You know you will be asked for an update by senior management at the most inappropriate time, so you should always be ready.

18

Monitoring Progress

INTRODUCTION

Have you ever heard this? 'What if I gave you a million dollars – could you do it then?'

It's a way of giving people the slight whack on the head they might need when they are sure that something can't be done. The right answer, if someone gave you a million dollars, might be that you'd quit the job and be sunning yourself on a beach somewhere. Seriously though, it might just remind you that there are some options that might work.

On one project, extra pay was given to a team of CAD designers to catch up on a backlog that was risking the entire project. They made a few thousand pounds extra, the project came in on time and it made several million for the company immediately.

Seems like a good deal, right? Well, you'd be surprised how often simple changes to existing practices can be difficult to get through the bureaucracy. As a project manager you need to be prepared to think far outside the box and solve the near impossible questions.

The harsh reality is that there are few times in a project when someone comes around with unlimited resources to help you out. Worse than that, you are likely to have some strong constraints on cash and other resources. Your project is likely to exist within the envelope of a number of other projects that are all competing for resources.

As I have said before, getting your project complete at the expense of other projects may not be the best solution for the company. Whenever possible you should 'play nice' by helping out other projects and recognize that sometimes the big decisions elsewhere will impact your own project negatively. Having a realistic and up-to-date plan will enable you to communicate the real impact of any such decisions as soon as they are made.

HOW TO MONITOR PROGRESS WITHIN A PROJECT

The challenge is that, as project manager, you have a budget and, to avoid blowing it all in the first few weeks, you need to know how to monitor the project effectively.

As a basis for many approaches to measuring progress, you need to have some idea of the cost of each resource. For physical resources, this might be:

- the cost recovery figure per hour/day/month;
- rental;
- hire cost;
- lease cost.

For individuals, the cost to the project will depend on where they are employed and the accounting practices within the company. External resources (consultants, contractors, labour) are relatively easy to price as their true cost is known.

For internal people, the cost can be harder to understand as there are often allocations of central costs (R&D, head office costs, etc). However, the accounts team within your company should be able to tell you the cost figures to use.

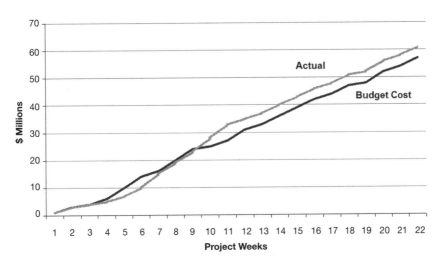

Figure 18.1 Actual vs budget spend by week

You might consider looking at the amount that is 'spent' on the project on a week-by-week basis, as shown in Figure 18.1.

It looks sensible doesn't it – slightly over budget but not wildly out of control?

Well, the problem you may have spotted is that the actual amount spent is monitored by time, not by achievements. The chart seems on track but the project could be lagging severely behind the timescales defined for it. That would mean that for the progress achieved, the project might be severely over-spent. As a project manager, the chart gives you no way of knowing whether things are going well or badly. It is useless.

Looking at the spend over time is unsatisfactory, so imagine that we looked at the spend per milestone. We might see something like the chart in Figure 18.2 (which arranges the milestones sequentially with any parallel milestones aggregated together in the chart).

You can see that up to milestone 5, the budget looks OK, then suddenly it is exceeded during completion of milestone 6.

One challenge here is that you do not plan a project to a high level of detail from start to finish in one hit. The rolling wave approach means that the plan may only be fully detailed in terms of resources

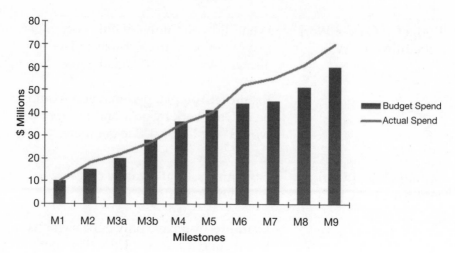

Figure 18.2 Actual vs budget spend by milestone

(and hence costs) one or two milestones in advance, after which it will be less detailed.

A more consistent approach to measuring progress is called 'earned value analysis'.

EARNED VALUE ANALYSIS (EVA)

EVA can seem a little intimidating, but it is mainly common sense. I'll go through the theory first, then show you some simple charts that really make it easy to keep on top of costs vs budgets.

EVA is an industry standard approach based on:

- measuring the progress of a project;
- forecasting completion date and cost;
- providing budget and schedule variances during the project.

The name comes from work being credited to the project or 'earned' as it is completed. It includes a number of different measurements that can be made regularly during the project; see Table 18.1.

Table 18.1 EVA measurements

Budgeted Cost of Work Scheduled (BCWS)	What did you think it would cost to get to a given point in the project? This is also known as the 'Planned value'.
	Example: You planned that you would be in New York by now and thought it would cost US $1,000 to get there.
Actual Cost of Work Performed (ACWP)	How much did it **actually** cost to do what you have done?
	Example: You have only gone as far as Boston and it has cost US $695 to get there.
Budgeted Cost of Work Performed (BCWP)	How much **should it have cost** to do what you have done? Also known as the 'Earned value'.
	Example: You have only got to Boston and **you thought it would cost** US $875 to get there.

These measurements can then be compared to see how the project is fairing against what was expected. Here are a few examples to help understand EVA better. Figure 18.3 shows a comparison of the budgeted and actual spend to get to this point in the project. Note that all the amounts are the cumulative spend to a point in the project.

In Figure 18.4, the budgeted cost of work scheduled to the end of the project is also shown. It is based on the actual cost of work performed to the current point in the project and represents the additional costs budgeted to get to completion from the current point. Notice the budgeted amount for the remaining work is added to the actual cost to date rather than what you expected to spend to this point. This is common sense to update the expected amount with what has actually happened to this point in the project.

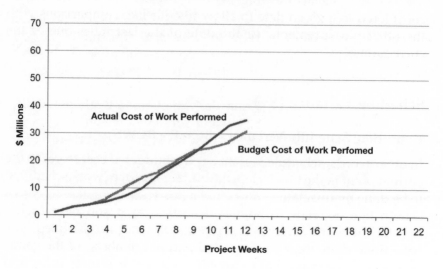

Figure 18.3 EVA – actual vs budget cost of work performed

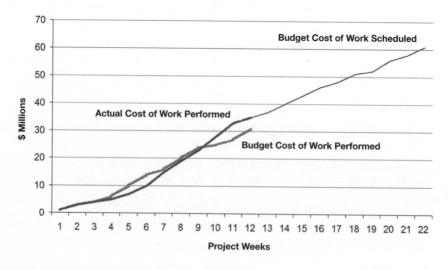

Figure 18.4 EVA – actual vs budget cost of work performed with budget cost for remaining work

When looking at the progress of a project, the BCWS will be considered to a given date to allow like-for-like comparisons with the other measurements, eg the date of the last milestone or the current date.

Schedule Variance (SV)

Definition: Schedule Variance = BCWP – BCWS

In other words, schedule variance is the budgeted cost to get to the current point in the project less the budgeted cost of work scheduled to be done by this date.

Both figures relate to budgeted figures, so if you have higher cost for the work performed compared to what is scheduled, you have done more than you expected and so are ahead of the game. Similarly, a negative value for SV means the project is behind schedule.

Cost Variance (CV)

Definition: Cost Variance = BCWP – ACWP

This is the budgeted cost of work performed less the actual cost to do the work that has been performed. In other words, for the same work planned, if the budget cost is greater than the actual cost then you are under budget (CV positive). Using the same logic, a negative value for CV means the project is over budget.

Schedule Performance Indicator (SPI)

Definition: Schedule Performance Indicator (SPI) = BCWP/BCWS

If the cost of the work scheduled is greater than the cost of the work performed then you are behind schedule (and the value of SPI will be below 1). If SPI is greater than 1 you are ahead of the schedule.

Cost Performance Indicator (CPI)

Definition: Cost Performance Index (CPI) = BCWP – ACWP

If the actual cost of the work performed is greater than the budgeted cost (for the same work) then the project is over budget and the CPI will be below 1.

Cost Schedule Index (CSI)

Definition: Cost Schedule Index (CSI) = CPI × SPI

The lower the value of the CSI below 1.0, the lower the probability that the project will be able to recover.

> Defence Acquisition University in the USA found that...
>
> When a project is 10 per cent complete, any overrun at project completion will not be less than at this particular point.
>
> When a project is 20 per cent complete, the CPI does not vary from the value at that point by more than 10 per cent. This means that if you are over budget at this point, it will be difficult to improve things dramatically. The reverse case does not follow the same logic as there is always room to go hideously over-spent if you don't pay attention.

USING EVA TO MONITOR PROGRESS

There's some complex theory there, but in practice using EVA can be very straightforward. Let's look at four simple cases to show how you can monitor cost and budget in a project using EVA principles but without too much pain.

In Figure 18.5, the planned cost of work completed is above the cost of work that was scheduled. This means that more work has been done at this point than expected, so **the project is ahead of schedule**.

The actual cost of work completed is below the planned cost for the work completed, so **the project is under-spent**.

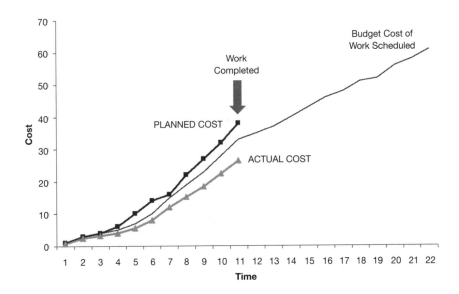

Figure 18.5 EVA example – project ahead of schedule and underspent

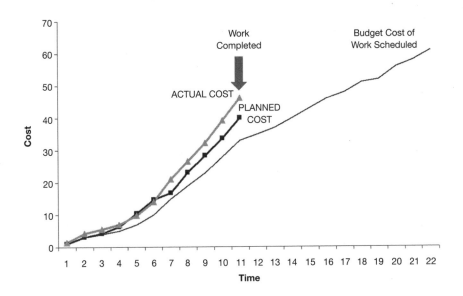

Figure 18.6 EVA example – project ahead of schedule and overspent

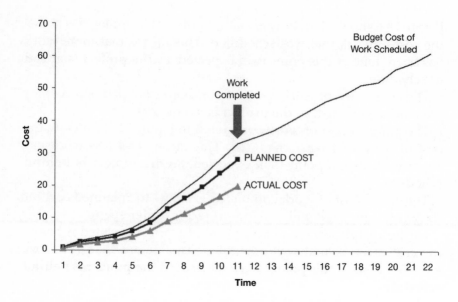

Figure 18.7 EVA example – project behind schedule and under-spent

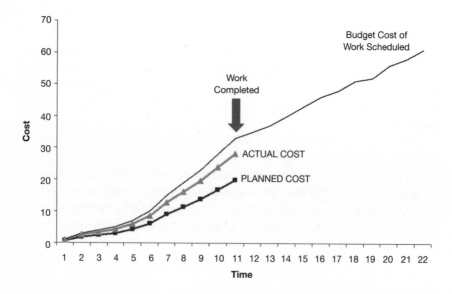

Figure 18.8 EVA example – project behind schedule and over-spent

Figure 18.6 shows that the planned cost of work completed is above the cost of work that was scheduled. This means that more work has been done at this point than expected, so **the project is ahead of schedule**.

The actual cost of work completed is above the planned cost for the work completed, so **the project is over-spent**.

The planned cost of work completed in Figure 18.7 is below the cost of work that was scheduled. This means that less work has been done at this point than expected, so **the project is behind schedule**.

The actual cost of work completed is below the planned cost for the work completed and so – **the project is under-spent**.

Figure 18.8 shows the planned cost of work completed is below the cost of work that was scheduled. This means that less work has been done at this point than expected, so **the project is behind schedule**.

The actual cost of work completed is above the planned cost for the work completed, so **the project is over-spent**.

LIMITATIONS OF EVA

A word of warning about using EVA. Tasks are only used in calculating the earned value graphs when they are complete. In practice you may find a significant number of tasks that are nearly, but not quite, completed. At these times the EVA will under-estimate the true progress of the project. There's no simple solution for this effect but it is significantly reduced if you plan in smaller chunks of work.

When you see issues from EVA analysis you should go back to the task information that has been used to create the figures. Identify tasks that should have been finished by now and investigate further to see if there are serious issues or this is a case of the analysis tool not reflecting reality. Much of the time you will be sufficiently on top of the project to be able to explain poor EVAs without much additional work.

19

Handling Issues

INTRODUCTION

No battle plan survives contact with the enemy. (Helmuth von Moltke)

This phrase is also true for projects. From the minute you start the project, things will start happening that you need to manage. Keeping on track in the face of the problems is the core of being a project manager. Remember, it's about getting to the destination, not getting there the way you originally intended. Flexibility and responsiveness to issues as they arise are going to be the key to success.

Issues and risks are different

You might be wondering why you need to deal with issues when we have already covered risk management at length. The simple explanation is that risks and issues are different:

- **risks** are things that may happen in the future and you need to eliminate, mitigate or avoid;
- **issues** have already happened.

WHAT IS AN ISSUE?

In simple terms, an issue is something that has occurred that threatens the successful completion of the project or provides an opportunity.

There are plenty of issues that can hurt a project, including:

- losing resources to other projects;
- realizing that a milestone may be missed;
- recognizing the likelihood that part of the specification cannot be met;
- encountering quality problems;
- customer requirements being changed.

There are also many positive opportunities that may present themselves during the life of a project. Either way, problem or opportunity, you need to handle the issue effectively and as early as practically possible.

PRIORITIZING ISSUES

Issues can be prioritized according to the example criteria shown in Table 19.1.

MANAGING ISSUES

There are a few basic principles to handling issues. You need to record them so that others involved in the project have a central location where they can check on the issues that exist, progress, etc. The log should include the following elements:

- Issue number – to help track particular issues easily.
- Description – including supporting document references.
- Date originated.
- Priority 1 to 3.
- Status – Identified, Investigation, Resolved.

- Comments – additional information about the resolution or exploitation of the issue.

Table 19.1 Example criteria for prioritizing issues

Priority	Response timing	Example issues
1	Immediate response	Project progress halted Immediate delay to the project Technical/quality 'showstopper' encountered Evidence that specification cannot be met under current plan Major shortcut to completion identified Cost/time reduction opportunity Test failures
2	Rapid response	Resourcing problems Changes of availability of equipment Potential delay
3	Respond when resources allow	Documentation errors

The issue list should be reviewed formally during the weekly meetings and updated as necessary. It may be that other issues appear and are resolved between meetings, because they are either too serious to wait or so simple they can be fixed easily and quickly. They should all be recorded to provide visibility of what has been handled and why certain decisions have been made.

20

Controlling Change

During the course of the project, there will need to be a number of changes. The project manager needs to strike a balance between protecting the project from unnecessary changes and potentially being uncooperative when changes are in the best interests of the organization.

It is important that there is a simple process in place to manage change and that you embrace change that is beneficial to the project.

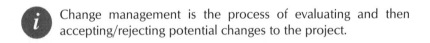 Change management is the process of evaluating and then accepting/rejecting potential changes to the project.

Changes within the project may originate from a variety of sources:

- failures in testing;
- customer requests/demands;
- response to competitor actions mid-project;
- issues – problems or opportunities;
- strategies to reduce risk;
- results of other projects.

When a potential change is highlighted, the project manager needs to record the details in a change log. This will capture who has raised the change, why they are suggesting it and when this was done.

The reason it is important to capture this information is to put the change into context. The customer **demanding** a difficult change is very different from a member of the project team **suggesting** it. The first case is normally dealt with by saying yes through gritted teeth, while the latter requires a rolled up copy of the project plan with which to beat the team member!

As well as stating the reason for the proposed change, any supporting documentation should be referenced – test results, customer specification, etc. The contents of a blank change log should look something like the example in Figure 20.1.

Number	Originator	Reason		Date originated	Impact assessment	Approval required from	Approved	Date	Comments	

Figure 20.1 Example change log

You need to start assessing what the impact of change would be in terms of additional cost, delays to the project's end date, increased risk, etc. Evaluating changes can end up generating considerable chunks of work in their own right. Frequently I have seen that the person needed to evaluate a change is also the person who is working flat out on the critical path of the project!

At this point you can decide against doing an impact assessment if you believe it is unnecessary or if you are going to reject the change. This is OK, but you need to record this in the change log and put your reasoning in the comments section.

If you choose to carry out an assessment, this work needs to be resourced and planned like the rest of the project.

Approving changes

A very minor change has no impact on the customer and so asking their opinion is frankly a waste of everyone's time. Similarly, you don't want a fundamental change to the project without ensuring that everyone is happy with it.

The logical approach is that different levels of approval are required depending on the impact of a proposed change, as shown in Table 20.1.

Table 20.1 Approval levels for change

The change...	Who can approve the change?	Actions
does not affect timescales	Project Manager alone	Record change in the change log
exceeds the acceptable contingency tolerances defined for the project (cost and/or timescales)	Project Sponsor	Submit change request form to the Project Sponsor Record decision in change log
fundamentally alters the agreed project definition (changing the specification and/or quality, significantly amending the budget or timescales)	Project Steering Group/Committee	Submit change request form to the Steering Group (via Project Sponsor) Record decision in change log

Note. These criteria should be decided before the start of the project. When the project is approved, there may have been some tolerances defined for aspects of the project. If the project goes outside these parameters in terms of time to completion, budget, etc, then the project manager may have to gain fresh approval from the project steering group to proceed. This may well generate a number of change requests that will need their approval, as applying them will break the defined tolerance limits.

In the change log, you should enter who is required to approve a particular change that has been proposed and their ultimate decision after any evaluation. This log is very useful as it provides a trail of how decisions were made, and the nature of the approval process means you aren't hanged when someone decides to disagree with one of the decisions later on.

Change request form

Figure 20.2 is an example of a change request form. Having information submitted and stored in a standard format ensures you have a record of all the information you need.

Change Request Form		
Project Name:		PCR No:
Proposed Change:		
Reason(s) for Change:		
Submitted By:		Date:
Man Days for Impact Assessment:		
Accept/Reject for Assessment	Project Manager	Date:
Reason:		
Impact of Change (with references):		
Assessment Valid Until:		
Requires Approval from:	(Project Manager or Project Sponsor or Steering Committee)	
Change Approved/Rejected:	Approved by:	Date:

Figure 20.2 Example change request form

21

Reporting

REPORTING DOWN

You should provide an overview of the state of the project to all team members on a regular basis. This is probably best done as a monthly update for long-duration projects but can be weekly if the project is shorter.

The update should include:

- current status within the milestone plan;
- significant events (eg passed a gate if the company runs a stage gate process);
- performance against budget;
- risks and mitigating factors relating to their part of the project.

Individual team members should see a copy of sections of the plan particular to what they are working on, with enough information to understand how their work fits into the broader context of the project.

REPORTING UP

You shouldn't provide the fully detailed project plan to senior management. The simple reason is that there will be too much information for them to digest and you really aren't providing them with meaningful information. They'll end up confused or concerned. Either way, they'll ask you more questions and unlikely to provide new resources or make changes when you need them. Not to mention the fact that senior management are going to question whether you have the right stuff to be a project manager.

Instead of providing 500 pages of lovingly detailed Gantt charts, the project manager should provide meaningful information to the project sponsor (and steering group if there is one) on a regular basis. Depending on the scale of the project, this information should be an appropriate selection from the following:

- project name;
- project objective (as defined with project team);
- project milestones;
- achievements in month (not activities);
- last tollgate passed;
- predicted date of next tollgate;
- last milestone passed;
- predicted date of next milestone;
- important upcoming activities;
- initial project budget;
- EVA summary;
- budget spent/committed to date;
- budget predicted to end of year (end of budget period);
- budget prediction to end of project;
- risk list – current list prioritized with proposed actions;
- progress on previous risks – management actions;
- key problems;
- decisions required by the project team (attach supporting information if necessary) – who takes decision, when, etc;
- next team meeting – details;
- file location of key documents.

22

Project Closure

It's strange, but few companies worry about how to close down projects.

A project may finish earlier than expected if it fails to pass an internal gate review or the project manager announces that it cannot meet the next milestone in spite of the team's best efforts. No matter how the project ends, it is important that the project is closed down properly.

The best way to close a project is with a meeting where the objectives of the project are reviewed against what has been delivered. Remember, a well-formed objective at the start of the project will help you measure whether the project has been a success (eg defined acceptance tests). The project sponsor can then sign off that the project is complete.

Post-project review

A second activity is to carry out a post-project review which:

- identifies useful lessons for the future that were learnt during the course of the project;

- helps identify what went wrong in the project and converts the pain experienced by the project team into learning for the organization;
- provides recognition of the achievements of the team.

The review should not spend time developing answers to the problems – just explain what the problems were. If it does not, the project team might spend time coming up with solutions to problems that are already being addressed elsewhere in the business. These issues *might* become new projects, but you don't want resources being 'lost' to the organization as they seek to answer the problems they encountered in completing the original project.

Team issues

Remember that some of your team may be sad to be at the end of the project. It might mean the end of their contract and certainly means the break-up of what could have become a very high performance and closely knit team. Some people cope badly with change and it will be a difficult time for them.

To help minimize these problems, try to identify the next project for your team if you can. This may mean talking to their resource managers to ensure they know that a person is becoming free and discussing what is coming up for him or her.

Freeing up resources as early as possible without risk to your project will gain you Brownie points from the resource managers. However, I advise against letting the team resources start on new projects while an element of risk remains within the current one. This is because the new project can rapidly become more interesting than the old project. The new project manager has more control over the future of team members, so if the new manager becomes demanding, it can be hard to resist responding.

In addition, take the time to write a message about the project for the company newsletter, intranet or as a global e-mail. In this you can point out the lessons learnt from the project and the contributions from members of your team. If they've done well, public praise can only help their careers and will also enhance your reputation for looking after your team.

Appendix 1: The Changing Nature of Projects

There have been challenging projects dating all the way back to the Egyptians. You can find pyramids where construction was abandoned when the sides were discovered to be too vertical to join up at a reasonable height, or that simply collapsed under their own weight. I suspect you might find more than one project manager buried under there too – either by accident or when the 'customer' found out about problems with construction.

The changes to the way we run projects are worth considering because of the impact on the project manager. You will not be surprised to read that projects are far more challenging than they used to be.

INCREASING LEGAL AND ADMINISTRATIVE OBLIGATIONS

Nearly 150 years ago, putting a railway across the United States had a human cost measured in the thousands. The sun beat down on the workers in summer, the cold killed them in winter, and dysentery and pneumonia weakened them in between. And as if this weren't bad enough, more deaths came from tunnel collapses and landslides, and accidents with the nitroglycerine needed to blast a path across the country.

Nowadays, we live in very different times in terms of the perceived value of human life. Deaths in major engineering projects are now rare and are genuinely shocking when they occur. In comparison to those historic railroad projects, 'only' eight people died on the UK side of the 31-mile Channel Tunnel project. This is an incredible project that links England and France for the first time since the last Ice Age, but even eight fatalities is still a hell of a price to pay.

Another illustration of how times have changed comes from the 'Big Dig' project in Boston. This is an awesome project to create a 10-lane underground highway to alleviate traffic congestion in the city. When one of the workers died due to a collapse within a tunnel, it was treated as major news.

The level of responsibility for those involved in projects has rocketed. As an example, directors of companies involved in a fatal accident may face corporate manslaughter charges. If those aren't laid against them, they may be hit by charges relating to breaches of health and safety regulations.

If you're not involved in this type of project, life's easier, right? Easier yes, but still likely to be far more complex than a few years ago. Product liability risks and increasingly litigious consumers mean that companies need to do more complex risk assessments and provide a trail of information that could be audited later on if things go wrong. In parallel, the ever spreading safety culture means we have increasingly stringent testing and standards for products.

Even if you don't make a product there are still more regulations to deal with. For example:

- training is required for employees and contractors to keep them safe on site;
- the use and storage of customer information is regulated in many countries and means most companies now need to comply with the rules;
- health and safety audits are needed to ensure teams in offices are even sitting correctly;
- project managers are increasingly being made responsible for assuring the mental health of their teams in addition to their physical well-being.

Whatever type of project you are running, you can guarantee the level of documentation and time spent considering health, safety and liability issues will be significantly higher than even 10 years ago.

INCREASING COMPLEXITY

The view in the 1960s was that technology would set us free. In fact, you'll have noticed you can't escape from work these days because of all the gadgets. Your mobile phone, pager, laptop, wireless communication, mobile broadband, BlackBerry, etc mean you can't escape by being away from your desk or going home for the day. If this isn't true for you, a lot of the readers of this book will want your job.

The result is that project managers can't escape from problems within their projects. At the same time, layered on the top of traditional problems is a trend of increasing globalization of companies, with more projects being run internationally. Software development may be in Mumbai or St Petersburg, a call centre in India, R&D centres in California, Israel and England. Some project managers arrive to catch up on issues e-mailed to them overnight, and are there 15 hours later on the phone to a country that has just woken up. A project may involve other divisions of the same company, joint venture partners, contractors and consultants – all with different agendas and different levels of accountability. Some are there for financial reasons, while others are involved because they have to be. Historic contracts may bind some very under-motivated people or companies into a project, and the project manager has to try to juggle all these elements to keep on track.

Collaborative tools have certainly improved over the years, enabling companies to share documents and work together in these larger, geographically spread, virtual teams. The tools are better, but nonetheless it is still a complex challenge to try to keep all these different elements working together effectively. In particular, you are deprived of some of the face-to-face time that can be invaluable in creating strong relationships and in spotting problems early.

That complexity isn't going away, so you might as well get used to it. One day you'll look back and think these days were the simple times – that's how fast things are going to continue to change.

INCREASING IMPACT OF TECHNOLOGY

If there's a technology aspect to your project, you can almost guarantee that it's more sophisticated than it used to be. Let's consider a few examples.

If you look at a Mercedes from the 1980s, there was bullet-proof engineering but little technology. Fast forward 20 years and customers (wealthy ones I admit) are driving Mercs with infra-red lighting, head-up displays, radar brake assistance, anti-lock brakes, traction control, etc. If I listed the acronyms for all the technology in a Mitsubishi Evo then there'd be no space for anything else in the book!

If we consider the evolution of computer processors, there is a trend that has been defined as Moore's Law. This suggested that computer processors would double the number of transistors (and hence their processing power) every 18 months. Amazingly, it has been pretty accurate from the early 1970s through to today. That's a fairly scary rate of progress, but it's only half as fast as the screaming development rate of the graphics processors that create the images on your computer monitor. As graphics capabilities have improved, the market's expectation for video game performance has also increased. The expanding storage capacity made available by using CDs, and then DVDs, means games have been bundled with ever larger video 'cut scenes' and environments to explore. The movement of characters has to be ever more realistic and so the movement of real people is captured and mapped into the software and the resolutions are climbing all the time.

That's a heavy combination of different technologies driving video games forward, and game development has moved from the bedroom project to multi-million dollar development in 20 years.

On the surface, there are some types of project that appear easier because of advances in computer-aided design and complex simulation. That is true if you keep doing problems with the same level of difficulty. However, these tools mean projects that were previously thought impossible are now being attempted:

- The Millau Bridge is the tallest bridge in the world with one pier actually taller than the Eiffel Tower.
- Denmark and Sweden are linked for the first time in 7,000 years by the incredible Øresund road and rail bridge.

- Boston is having an incredible 10-lane road network built under the city to relieve congestion.

Just when you think life will get simpler due to technology, someone decides to go higher, faster, deeper, and creates ever bigger and more financially mind-boggling projects.

INCREASING IMPACT OF CULTURE

Globalization doesn't mean that we're all the same – even if McDonalds seems to be everywhere. When working across borders you will have to take account of the differences in culture and approach.

In Germany and Switzerland you will find that the specification phase for anything is much longer than in the UK, United States or Far East. If you try to rush them, you will face a real uphill struggle. They want to produce a very detailed, low-risk, high detail spec, and I've been grateful, and occasionally frustrated, for that on many occasions.

If you want to work with the Dutch then you will probably have to get used to some of them having 43 days holiday a year. Conversely, when you work with Americans you will wish they took more holidays so you can take a break from time to time.

You could try to bully the Swedes, but the strong social security system there means there is little fear involved in losing their job.

In the early 1990s I saw a very famous industrialist and TV personality tell a group of Swedish engineers that they were all lazy and that he had Chinese engineers who could do the same job for a third of the cost and with twice the output. Needless to say this didn't go down well. and was one of the least thought out attempts at 'motivating' a team I have ever seen.

ERRORS GO A LOT FURTHER THAN BEFORE

Classic marketing thinking used to be that if someone liked a product they would tell three people, but if they didn't they'd tell 11. These days the internet means that bad news travels much more quickly and far more widely. Chances are you heard about the 2005 issues with the screen of the iPod Nano or the 2006 recall of Dell/Apple laptops due to faulty Sony batteries that could catch fire.

Newsgroups, chat rooms, online forums and blogs mean that if you've screwed up, people will find out faster and the bad news will be accessible globally. A bad project can now stall your career faster than you'd believe – even if it wasn't your fault. In the same vein, companies can be embarrassed by problems far more than they were in the past – and hell hath no fury like an embarrassed executive, I can assure you.

The result of all this is there's almost nowhere you can hide these days. There's not a lot you can do about it, but I wanted to cheer you up before tackling the next appendix.

Appendix 2: Project Management Software

This book is not going to explain how to use project management software. Theses packages normally have tutorials built in, or are so fearsomely expensive that nice people in suits will come and train you in your office. If you get really desperate, there's probably a 'Dummies' book out there for you as well. However, it is useful to understand some of the strengths and weaknesses of software in action.

Before we start, let's consider something for a second. Do people who learn Microsoft Excel magically become economists overnight? I don't think so. I can just about use a chisel without removing several of my own body parts, but that doesn't mean I am Michelangelo. The same principle applies to project management software. Being able to use Microsoft Project doesn't turn someone into a good project manager! This book is about having the right approach first – then using software to support you. That's why this discussion is here as an appendix and not at the start!

Note: I tend to use examples from Microsoft Project because I like it and it is widely used, but the information below and throughout the book is true for most packages.

GANTT AND PERT CHARTS

The first thing to remember is why you have charts showing the project plan at all. Their purpose is to help you, as project manager, understand the relationship between different tasks and the effect of change on the project. The dependencies created between tasks, the resources available and the way these are applied will have an effect on the project plan that can clearly be seen using software.

In particular, software enables you to carry out 'what if' scenarios to understand the impact of proposed changes to the resourcing, specification and timing. The charts are also crucial in helping you optimize the first 'realistic' version of the plan that you create – identifying ways that you can improve the plan by altering the relative ordering of tasks, resources applied, etc.

Throughout this book, and in real life, I tend to display projects visually using timelines (Gantt charts). This is because they provide me with what I need when I look at a project. However, there are other views of the same information that you may prefer or want to use in certain circumstances.

To help you decide which to use when, the following section describes two popular approaches in more detail and discusses their strengths and weaknesses.

Gantt charts

This type of representation is named after Henry Gantt and was based on his ideas from nearly 100 years ago. However, it took until the advent of the computer for it to really take off, as far more complex plans and relationships could be represented, as shown in Figure A2.1.

The duration of a task is represented by a box drawn against a linear timescale. The start of the task is the left-hand edge of the box, and the right-hand side is the end of the task. The timescale can be changed to show days, weeks, months, etc. This allows the user to zoom in or out on different sections of the plan to look more closely at the relationships represented in the chart.

To the left of the chart, you can display more or less any information relating to the project that you need. You almost always want to see the task names, but you can configure the view to show the

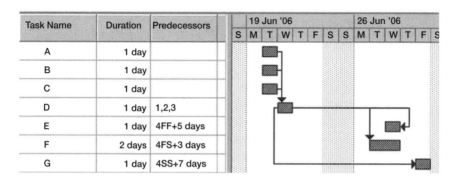

Task Name	Duration	Predecessors	19 Jun '06							26 Jun '06						
			S	M	T	W	T	F	S	S	M	T	W	T	F	S
A	1 day															
B	1 day															
C	1 day															
D	1 day	1,2,3														
E	1 day	4FF+5 days														
F	2 days	4FS+3 days														
G	1 day	4SS+7 days														

Figure A2.1 Example Gantt chart

resources, duration, predecessors, successors, etc relating to each task.

Gantt charts are very good at representing the relationship between tasks and sub-tasks. In Figure A2.2, B is a summary task made up of three sequential sub-tasks. You can see that in Microsoft Project (below), B is shown as a black bar with downward triangles that mark the start of the first sub-task and the end of the last sub-task. In addition, the task names of the sub-tasks are indented one level to the right.

In Figure A2.3, the task B3 is further divided into two sub-tasks B31 and B32.

Task Name	Duration	Predecessors	19 Jun '06								26 Ju	
			S	S	M	T	W	T	F	S	S	M	T
A	1 day											
⊟ B	3 days	1										
B1	1 day											
B2	1 day	3										
B3	1 day	4										
C	1 day	5										

Figure A2.2 Gantt chart showing summary tasks and tasks

Task Name	Duration	Predecessors	19 Jun '06							26 Jun '06			
			M	T	W	T	F	S	S	M	T	W	T
A	1 day												
⊟ B	4 days	1											
B1	1 day												
B2	1 day	3											
⊟ B3	2 days	4											
B31	1 day												
B32	1 day	6											
C	1 day	7											

Figure A2.3 Gantt chart showing summary tasks, tasks and sub-tasks

You can see that the task B3 now has a black bar marking from the start of B31 to the end of B32. However, B3 is still a sub-task of B and you can see that the bar marking B has extended to cover until the end of B3. B31 and B32 are indented twice relative to B to show they are sub-tasks of a sub-task of B.

To improve clarity, tasks can be grouped into sections that represent different logical parts of the project and then listed close to the order in which they will start. This makes it easier to see which tasks relate to each other and also the flow of tasks through the project – see Figure A2.4.

Task Name	Duration	Start	WBS	Predecessors	July 2006										
					17	20	23	26	29	02	05	08	11	14	17	20	23
⊟ Design	14 days	Tue 20/06/06	1												
Specification	5 days	Tue 20/06/06	1.1												
CAD drawing	2 days	Tue 27/06/06	1.2	2											
Verification	7 days	Thu 29/06/06	1.3	3											
⊟ Modelling	10 days	Mon 10/07/06	2	4											
Build initial version	10 days	Mon 10/07/06	2.1												
⊟ Marketing	17 days	Tue 20/06/06	3												
Design packaging	5 days	Tue 20/06/06	3.1												
Get quotations	10 days	Tue 27/06/06	3.2	8											
Decide on supplier	2 days	Tue 11/07/06	3.3	9											

Figure A2.4 Gantt chart with tasks organized into logical categories

Advantages of Gantt charts

- Excellent for showing scheduling of tasks within the project.
- Very flexible display of information relating to each task.
- Can automatically display the critical path for the project.

Disadvantages of Gantt charts

- Looking at larger projects on the screen can become tricky as you have to scroll up and down through the task list.
- Can be difficult to identify relationships when there are many tasks and dependencies and the Gantt view becomes more cluttered.

PERT charts

Project Evaluation and Review Technique (PERT) charts date back to the time before computers when a project plan would be paper-based. PERT charts can be configured to display a variety of information in a box that represents each task. Figure A2.5 shows a PERT chart view of a project plan.

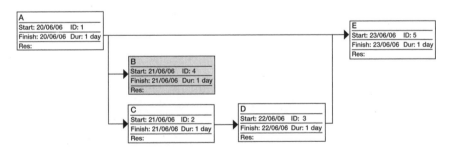

Figure A2.5 Example PERT chart

Each box contains important information about a particular task. Figure A2.6 shows an individual task with the name, duration and start and finish dates incorporated in the box.

In Microsoft Project a task box is displayed as shown in Figure A2.7.

	Activity		
Task Number	1	32	Duration
Start Date	31/8/06	17/09/06	Finish Date

Figure A2.6 A PERT chart task box

Example
Start: 25/09/06   ID: 1
Finish: 25/09/06 Dur: 1 day
Res:

Figure A2.7 A PERT chart task box as displayed in Microsoft Project

The dependencies between different tasks are shown by an arrow between the boxes. In some packages, the position of the line relative to the task box indicates the type of dependency between the tasks – eg start to finish. The information displayed in each task box can be selected by the user. The one chosen could also show resources allocated to a task, for example.

The task number always seems superfluous when you have the name of the task, but remember the PERT chart ordering will not necessarily be identical to the ordering of the tasks when viewed as a task list. It can be a pain to try to search through a long list of activities to find the right task name, so I tend to keep the task number visible so I can quickly refer back to the task list if I need to.

There are a few things to note. A major point is that the duration of a task is not indicated visually except by a number in the box. If you are used to working with timelines where the duration is proportional to the length of each task bar, this can seem quite strange. The box for a one-day task is the same size as that for a 100 man-year task. This can make it difficult to quickly identify larger tasks within the plan.

The second issue is how sub-tasks are treated in the PERT chart view. Every task has a box created for it when it is added to a project. However, if you have a very complicated plan with many sub-tasks at different levels of detail, it can become tricky to understand where you are in the structure of the plan. An example is the best way to illustrate this problem.

If I have three tasks that are consecutive, I can represent them as A, B and C and a PERT chart would show them as three boxes neatly in a line with A leading to B and B leading to C. This is shown in Figure A2.8.

A
Start: 20/06/06 ID: 1
Finish: 20/06/06 Dur: 1 day
Res:
B
Start: 21/06/06 ID: 2
Finish: 21/06/06 Dur: 1 day
Res:
C
Start: 22/06/06 ID: 3
Finish: 22/06/06 Dur: 1 day
Res:

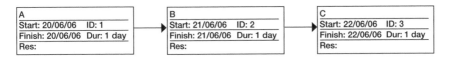

Figure A2.8 A PERT chart view of three consecutive tasks

Now imagine that task B requires further detail and we create some sub-tasks for it. B1, B2 and B3 are all sequential tasks that contribute to the completion of B. In other words, the actual order of tasks is now A, B1, B2, B3, C. Let's look at the Gantt chart for this to make it clearer; see Figure A2.9.

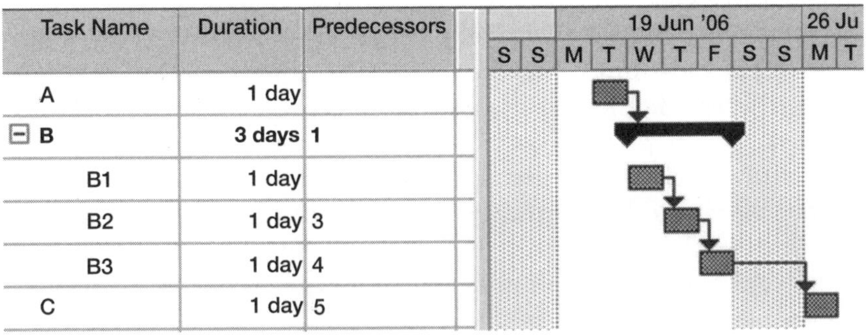

Task Name
Duration
Predecessors
19 Jun '06
26 Ju
S S M T W T F S S M T
A
1 day
B
3 days
1
B1
1 day
B2
1 day
3
B3
1 day
4
C
1 day
5

Figure A2.9 Gantt chart showing sub-tasks for task B

Microsoft Project displays these same tasks as a PERT chart, as shown in Figure A2.10.

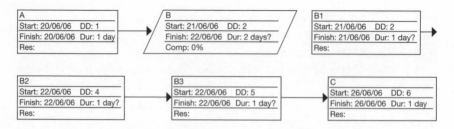

Figure A2.10 PERT chart with sub-tasks for task B

I can't see which task is which if I zoom out to see all the tasks, but I can't see the relationships if I zoom in! The diagram shows B as a summary task that starts when B1 starts, and is complete when B3 finishes, but you can only take my word for it!

As soon as you get complexity in a PERT chart you start to generate problems with what links to what level of task and what you do with all the other tasks that are not linked into the chart. Trust me, this way lies madness. Some people swear by PERT charts, I just tend to swear at them!

Advantages of PERT charts

- Can be used to create useful overviews of project progress.
- Can be easier to follow the relationships between tasks than a timeline-type view where the plan has a morass of vertical and horizontal lines.

Disadvantages of PERT charts

- No visual representation of task duration.
- Sometimes hard to read full task name within size constraints of the task box.
- The structure of the chart may fall apart and need correcting when new tasks are added or dependencies changed.
- No dates in background to provide sense of progress.
- Non-linear. A box may be one day or one year, so progressing from task box to task box is hard to understand in the context of the project.

Appendix 3: Project Management Approaches and Methodologies

There have been various attempts to standardize the approach to project management. The main driver for these has been the desire to reduce the late delivery and overspending in projects. A number of these frameworks try to limit the exposure of organizations by creating clear processes which, when applied, will cap the risk in a project. Others aim to overcome the challenges in notoriously difficult areas, eg software.

This chapter will describe a number of different methodologies/standards including the United States-centric *Project Management Book of Knowledge*, PRINCE2® from the UK, 'agile' software development methods, and ISO 10006.

Project Management Book of Knowledge (PMBOK)

PMBOK is under continual development by the Project Management Institute. It aims to capture the sum of knowledge within the world of project management. Initially published in 1987, the book is now in its third iteration and is also defined in a standard (IEEE 1490, 2003). The book acts as a reference guide, identifying and describing 'best practice' approaches that can be applied across all projects.

PMBOK is designed to be widely applicable across different types of project and contains five processes and nine knowledge areas. The process areas, each with sub-processes within them, are as follows:

- initiating;
- planning;
- executing;
- controlling and monitoring;
- closing.

It is clear that these processes are not discrete and there are important interactions between the planning, executing and controlling/monitoring processes.

The nine knowledge areas are:

- Project Integration Management.
- Project Scope Management.
- Project Time Management.
- Project Cost Management.
- Project Quality Management.
- Project Human Resource Management.
- Project Communications Management.
- Project Risk Management.
- Project Procurement Management.

PMBOK® is a registered trademark of the Project Management Institute.

PRINCE2®

Overview

The first version of the PRINCE (**PR**ojects **IN** Controlled Environments) methodology was developed by the UK government in

1989. It was designed to provide a standardized approach to the management of IT projects, but use of PRINCE has been expanded to cover many types of project in both the public and the private sector with the introduction of PRINCE2®. This second iteration builds on the original, but is more generic at the cost of some of the detail relating to software projects.

The PRINCE2® methodology is designed to allow management of extremely complex projects with massive budgets. The downside of this is that the processes are excessively detailed and onerous for many smaller projects. To allow for this, the elements of PRINCE2® include the concept of scalability so that the level of adoption can be tailored for the individual project.

Starting Up a Project (SU)

This is the first step in a PRINCE2® managed project and is the start of an implementation phase.

A top-down approach is taken with the project board/executive and sponsor identified prior to selecting a suitable project manager. A team is then assembled around the project manager, including project assurance and change control roles.

A Project Brief is then prepared by the project manager and the team, as well as a definition of the approach to be taken (contract out, perform in-house, etc). The aim of this work is that the Project Brief will be accepted and the project can proceed to the creation of a more detailed Project Initiation Document. This approach means you do not commit to creating hugely detailed initiation documents for every potential project.

Initiating a Project (IP)

In this phase of work, a more detailed business case is created.

The quality standards to be used are identified and then outline plans drawn up to support the business case – including timescales and estimated resource usage to completion. At this stage, a number of the project control and reporting mechanisms are established. These include the Issues Log that will be used during the life of the project, and the Lessons Learned Log that will capture experience from the project and help improve how future projects are run.

The final step is the creation of the Project Initiation Document for review before the project can pass to the next stage.

Planning (PL)

Once a planning tool has been identified, the PL process identifies the management 'products' and project outputs that will be necessary. A management product is something produced during the course of the project which is solely intended to help manage the project rather than directly help move it along. These outputs are broken down into work packages that are estimated. A risk assessment is also carried out on the work to be done and the Risk Log updated as necessary.

Once a software version of the plan is created, tolerances are agreed with the Project Board. These are the margins within which the project manager has authority to operate. If the project deviates beyond these margins then escalation is necessary.

Directing a Project (DP)

This process describes how the Project Board manages and controls the project during its life cycle. This process begins with a formal meeting to decide if the project should pass to the initiation phase. The Project Board also has the formal task of approving (or otherwise) the Project Initiation Document.

During the life of the project, the board defines the tolerance margins allowable during each phase and can authorize variations when the project goes beyond these margins. The Project Board can stop a project if quality falls below acceptable standards or if the business case no longer makes sense to the organization.

The DP process also describes how ad hoc direction can be given within the project and how project closure should take place.

Controlling a Stage (CS)

The Controlling a Stage process describes how each stage should be controlled during the project. It includes how work will be allocated combined with the quality checks that will be applied to this work.

It is particularly important in that it captures business and technical issues for both change control purposes and to understand any potential impact on the business case. The status of the project is reviewed to consider factors including progress against plan, risks and resources. The output of this review can be that everything is proceeding satisfactorily. However, if this is not the case, the CS process defines how corrective action should be taken for minor deviations. Where major deviations have taken place, this process incorporates escalation of the problem as an Exception Report.

Managing Product Delivery (MP)

This process is like a small version of the Controlling a Stage (CS) process. It deals with the allocation and acceptance of work packages within a stage. Progress of a work package is reviewed via checkpoint meetings and reports. If there is a risk of the work package exceeding the tolerances set by the Project Board, this is escalated to the Project Manager.

Each work package is defined with approval criteria at the start. When approved against these criteria, the Project Manager is informed that the work package has been completed.

Managing Stage Boundaries (SB)

At the boundary between stages, it is important to consider whether the business case for the project still makes sense. This means that the next stage should be reviewed and project plans updated with information from the current stage (time, costs, etc) and also from any exception plans created when the project has exceeded its tolerance margins. The business case should be updated to reflect the current information on costs, risks, benefits and timescales.

An End Stage Report is then produced to mark the end of the stage. This report includes the performance to date in terms of costs, resources used and the timescales needed to reach this point. The current status of major issues is also included. Figure A3.1 shows how the SB process looks when drawn as an IDEF-style process.

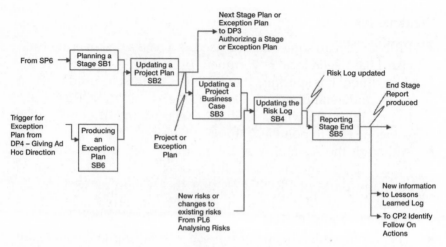

Figure A3.1 Example IDEF-style chart of the SB process

Closing a Project (CP)

Any further work or actions are captured at this point, and the Lessons Learned Report is generated from the information recorded during the life of the project.

A Post-project Review is set up to evaluate performance of the project against targets and to define how and when any measurements should be taken to input into this process. Finally, an End Project Report is produced with reference to the Project Initiation Document.

Strengths

- PRINCE2® is an open standard that can be applied by any organization without licence fees.
- It incorporates appropriate escalation of issues to senior management alongside the principle of 'management by exception'. This means management become involved with the project when necessary, rather then interfering with every minor detail.
- The scalability means PRINCE2® can be applied to a wide range of projects in terms of their complexity, budget, etc.
- PRINCE2® acts as a guide for the implementation of a project with a clear sequence of events from start-up to closure.
- Documentation is standardized – reducing training requirements and simplifying the integration of new members into the team.

Weaknesses

- PRINCE2® can sometimes be used as a backside-covering exercise. I have seen local government projects in the UK where the department has specified that PRINCE2® must be used without really understanding why. Defining the use of PRINCE2® seems to provide them with a feeling of security that they will have someone else to point at if things go wrong.
- Although the scalability of the methodology is necessary and useful, it also means that some projects effectively opt out of so many parts of PRINCE2® that they might as well not be following any of it. These are sometimes referred to as PINOs (Prince In Name Onlys).
- The approach is document-intensive – leading to a significant overhead of time required to produce reports and information that do not directly contribute to the completion of the project. These documents are sometimes called management 'products'. If there are no additional resources available for the project, delivering these management products can lead to longer project phases and overall duration.
- Even allowing for the scalability of some processes, PRINCE2® can still mean there is 'too much structure' overlaying the project compared to 'agile' methodologies.

PRINCE2® is a Registered Trade Mark of the Office of Government Commerce in the UK.

PMBOK® and PRINCE2® compared

PRINCE2® and *PMBOK®* cannot be directly compared as one is a methodology for running a project (PRINCE2), whereas the other is a detailed description of the knowledge necessary to be a project manager *(PMBOK)*. In simple terms, PRINCE2® is a checklist suited to running a project, whereas *PMBOK* is a reference guide designed to teach project managers. This means that learning PRINCE2® alone omits the details of some aspects of project management compared to the *PMBOK.*

PRINCE2® is very much focused on the life cycle of a project. The majority of processes follow the thread from Starting Up a Project through to Closing a Project. In contrast, the *PMBOK* is more functionally based and describes roles and outputs.

PRINCE2® concentrates on the implementation elements of a project and assumes aspects such as contract negotiation are separate activities. The *PMBOK* is a more complete project management approach that covers more of the life of a project than PRINCE2® – running from feasibility stages through to completion.

A number of organizations combine *PMBOK*-based training with the PRINCE2® approach to running projects.

AGILE DEVELOPMENT

Software projects are infamous for being difficult to project manage. The main problems seem to come from difficulties in estimating the amount of work required to complete parts of the code (modules). It has been recognized that methods such as PRINCE2® and *PMBOK* are not ideally suited to software development and a number of more flexible approaches have been developed.

'Predictive' approaches, as in this book, try to understand and define the future in detail. In contrast, agile development method-ologies aim to adapt work quickly to rapidly changing situations. They assume things will change so fast that planning in detail is a waste of effort and replace this with excellent communication and flexibility.

An agile team may only have detailed the work for the upcoming week. Work in the following month may be defined as new features and bug fixes to be incorporated. This is clearly a much lower level of detail of task and resource planning than would be seen in a 'traditional' planning approach.

This new approach to development is often credited to the creation of the 'Agile Manifesto'. This was written in 2001 and describes principles that are at the heart of most agile methodologies.

Manifesto for Agile Software Development

We are uncovering better ways of developing software by
doing it and helping others do it. Through this work we have
come to value:
Individuals and interactions over processes and tools
Working software over comprehensive documentation
Customer collaboration over contract negotiation
Responding to change over following a plan
That is, while there is value in the items on
the right, we value the items on the left more.

Using an agile approach means that software iterations are delivered
more frequently than in traditional development projects. Instead
of months, there could be a new release daily. This creates issues
with the ability to test the software, and the desirability of such an
approach will depend on whether you are updating live software
used by clients or internal development releases.

The lack of formality of documentation in the project means
communication becomes even more important, and the ability to
have frequent discussions with the involvement of customers is
vital.

Agile methods can work well in software development when:

- Programmers are experienced and used to working in an agile
  way.
- The team is small and preferably in the same location. Ideally,
  you don't want a floor or a wall between parts of the team. The
  more difficult it becomes to hold discussions within the team,
  the more problematic the project will become.
- There is constant access to the 'customer.'
- Requirements are changing rapidly.

Agile methods are less suited to situations where:

- The team is large (>20) or where smaller teams are not in the
  same location.
- The organizational culture cannot support devolving responsibility to individual programmers.

- Program management techniques concentrate on long-term budgetary and resource-based planning.
- There are mission-critical projects involved.
- The average programmer is relatively inexperienced or uncomfortable with this approach.
- Requirements are very stable.
- There is only limited risk of problems in delivering the software.

ISO 10006

In recognition of the important role of quality in projects, the International Standards Organization has developed ISO 10006: Guidelines for Quality Management in Projects.

The standard is very closely related to parts of the *Project Management Book of Knowledge* as the latter document was used heavily during drafting of the standard. However, ISO stresses that ISO 10006 is not a guide to project management itself. This reflects the criticism that the standard goes into great detail about some aspects of project management whilst providing insufficient information on others. ISO 10006 is therefore probably best used as an additional tool to benchmark performance in some project areas.

Unlike ISO 9002, for example, ISO 10006 is not intended to be used as a tool for registration or certification.

Appendix 4: Problem-solving Techniques

There are a number of different techniques to help you get to the causes of issues in a project or generate new solutions to a problem. Here are a couple you may find useful.

ISHIKAWA DIAGRAMS

Ishikawa or Fishbone Diagrams are different names for the same useful tool for helping identify potential causes leading to a problem or a desired effect.

To demonstrate how you create one of these diagrams, you start with the problem or the effect that you want to achieve. The following example is a real situation from a major infrastructure company.

First you create a horizontal arrow (the spine) pointing to the 'effect' being considered. In this case it is project management issues. Then you work either alone or with the team to brainstorm major causes that could create the effect. These are added to the diagram as diagonal 'bones' that join onto the spine; see Figure A4.1.

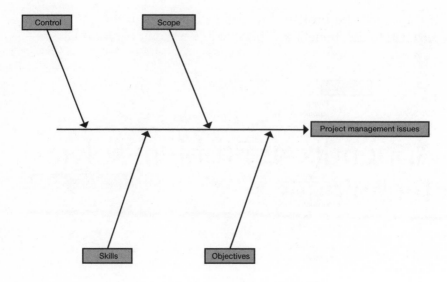

Figure A4.1 Start of an Ishikawa diagram to discover causes of issues in project management

You then add a further level of causes attached to the respective major cause.

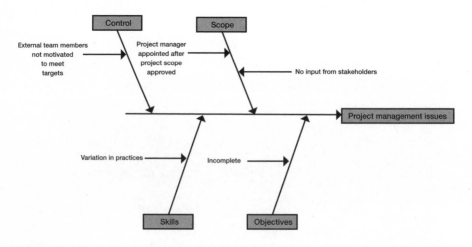

Figure A4.2 Adding detail to the potential causes of the problem

If causes can be broken down into more detail, these should be attached to the 'bone' they relate to as shown in Figure A4.3.

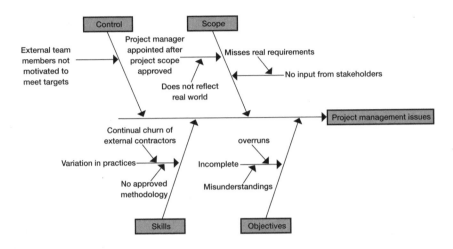

Figure A4.3 Fully detailed Ishikawa diagram for the project management problems

You may need to reorganize the diagram to move common elements together, or possibly split the diagram in two if it becomes too complex.

THE 'FIVE WHYS'

This is a very simple technique but one that is very useful when you are faced with someone telling you that something can't be done. It is also good at getting to the root of an issue fast.

The technique is this – just keep asking 'Why'? By asking why five times, you will quickly get below the surface and move the individual or team back from the effect to the causes. There may be a number of answers at any point, so you may need to follow each of these back until you've asked the question five times.

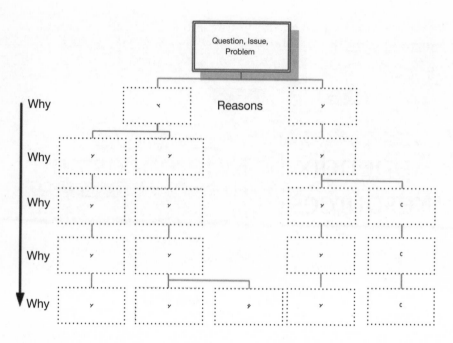

Figure A4.4 'Five Whys' approach

Appendix 5: References and Resources

REFERENCES

Chapter 5: McLaren and Bugatti case study from interviews in *Car, Magazine*, EMAP

Chapter 6: John F Kennedy speech available from www.jfklibrary. org

RECOMMENDED READING AND USEFUL RESOURCES

The Handbook of Project Based Management, (1998) J R Turner, McGraw-Hill

Prince2 Information, The Office of Government Commerce [Online] http://www.ogc.gov.uk/

PMBOK Information, Project Management Institute [Online] http://www.pmi.org

ACKNOWLEDGEMENTS

Microsoft product screen shot(s) reprinted with permission from Microsoft Corporation.

Index

95% complete   103

activities   85
Actual Cost of Work Performed
    (ACWP)   187
administrative obligations   205
'agile' software
    development   219
agreeing objectives   57
approving changes   199
assigning resources   96
assigning resources by role
    97
assumptions   39
availability   114
    baseline hours   116
    holidays   117
avoidance   41

bad milestones   67
bad project managers   33–34
    micro-manager   33
    panicker   34

Vegas project manager   14
baseline hours   116
'Big Dig' project, Boston   206
BlackBerry   207
'blame-finger'   43
blogs   210
budget   52
Budgeted Cost of Work
    Performed (BCWP)   187
Budgeted Cost of Work
    Scheduled (BCWS)   187
Bugatti Veyron   54
building a house   131

change approval   199
change log   198–200
    example   198
change management   197
    definition   197
change requests   200
    form   200
Channel Tunnel   206
checklist (for project

manager)   175–77
closing a project   203
collaborative tools   207
communication
    daily briefings   173
    perception   175
    phone conferences   173
    weekly meetings   172
company related risk   144
conflict   41, 168
constraint   28, 154, 156
contingency   12, 52, 91, 106,
    136, 137, 143, 147, 160, 162,
    199
    problems with contingency
        planning   137
contractors   98
controlling change   197
core project team   46
cost over-runs   74
Cost Performance Indicator
    (CPI)   189
Cost Schedule Index (CSI)   190
Cost Variance (CV)   189
crash table   161
crashing a project   119, 160
criteria based decision
    making   71
critical path   131–33, 135,
    153–58, 182, 198, 215
    identifying tasks on the
        critical path   132
    removing holes   153
culture   209
customers   50

death by content   11
Defence Acquisition University,
    190
definition team   46

dependencies   124
definition   124
    finish to finish   126
    finish to start   125
    lag   126
    predecessors   128
    start to start   125
    successors   128
dependency   124–26, 135, 153,
    216
diagnostic
    achievable and
        consistent   25
    believing the plan   24
    external inputs   25
    logic   25
    managing work   23
    multi-company
        programme   28
    objective   22
    other calls on time   23
    project plan   22
    realistic resourcing   25
    unrealistic constraints   27
'don't shoot the messenger'   9
doomed team   10
duration   5, 24, 26–28, 99, 100,
    103–04, 106–07, 109–11,
    114–15, 118–20, 122, 124,
    130, 132, 142, 147, 152–54,
    156–58, 160–61, 163, 182,
    201, 212–13, 215–16, 218,
    225
    most probable   109
    optimistic   109
    pessimistic   109
    weightings   110

Earned Value Analysis, *see* EVA
Eiffel Tower   208

Empire State Building   69
estimating duraction
   large teams   114
estimation
   95% complete   103
   complex estimation
      techniques   108
   dealing with differences in
      approach   102
   differing assumptions   101
   effect of adding
      resources   121
   estimates not updated   101
   how far to walk   104
   optimistic, pessimistic and
      probable durations
      111
   over-confidence   101
   percentage complete doesn't
      work   102
   problems with   106
   producing good
      estimates   108
   recording assumptions   111
   up to date   102
   who should be involved
      101
   why it goes wrong   100
EVA   186
   Actual Cost of Work
      Performed (ACWP)   187
   Budgeted Cost of
      Work Performed
      (BCWP)   187, 189
   Budgeted Cost of Work
      Scheduled (BCWS)   187,
      189
   Cost Performance Indicator
      (CPI)   189
   Cost Schedule Index

   (CSI)   190
   Cost Variance (CV)   189
      examples   190
      limitations   193
   Schedule Performance
      Indicator (SPI)   189
   Schedule Variance (SV)
      189
'everything goes right'
   plans   12
Excel   98, 181, 211
expected duration see most
   probable duration

F22 Raptor   145
finish to finish   134
finish to finish
   dependencies   126
finish to start   134
finish to start (FS)
   dependencies   125
fishbone diagrams   229
Five Whys, The   231
float   133, 135
focusing attention   41
   avoidance   41
   overtalking   42
   using silence   42
free slack   133

Gantt, Henry   212
Gantt charts   155, 202, 212,
   217
   disadvantages   215
   advantages   215
gate processes   72
gates   72
General Accounting Office
   (GAO)   146
good milestones   68

head up displays   208
how far is there to go   105

identifying risks   137
ignored team   9
impact   139, 146
impact of culture   209
impact of technology   208
incompetent team   9
increasingly complexity
     (projects)   207
initialization   44
injection moulding
     (example)   158
Ishikawa diagrams   229
ISO 10006   219, 228
issue definition   195
issue log   195
  response type   196
issue number   65, 195
issues   194
  differences compared to
       risks   194
  log   195
  managing   195
  number   65, 195
  prioritizing   195

Joint Strike Fighter   74

'keep it simple stupid'   44
Kipling, Rudyard   61
knowledge areas
     (PMBOK)   220

lag   126–29, 134–35, 153–54
leading projects   33
legal obligations   205
levelling   152, 154
limitations of EVA   193

management information
     202
managing issues   195
managing risks   137
matrix management   36
McDonalds   209
McLaren F1   54
measure of quality   70, 74
Mercedes   208
methodologies   219
micro-manager   33
Microsoft Project   26, 67, 111,
     129, 130, 211, 213, 216–17
milestone   8, 16, 54, 66– 71,
     73–75, 78, 81–83, 87, 89, 93,
     131, 168, 170, 185, 187, 195,
     201–03
  bad milestones   67
  characteristics compared to
       gates   73
  gates – comparison   70
  good milestones   68
  measurable   70
  outcomes   70
  refining   76
  states of achievement   68
  sub-milestones   82
  well defined   66
  writing   70
milestone statements
  examples   67
Millau Bridge   208
mitigation   136
Mitsubishi Evo   208
mobile broadband   207
module managers   169
monitoring progress   179, 183
  how to   184
Moore's Law   208
most probable duration   109

National Audit Office   74
New York City   69
newsgroups   210
nuclear submarines   40

Øresund road and rail
    bridge   208
objectives
  achievable   60
  agreeing   57
  attainable   60
  importance   57
  project intitiation
      objectives   47
  realistic   60
  relevant   66
  smart   59–60
  timed   60
  unambiguous   58
  well defined   59
online fora   210
optimization   158
optimizing   151
optimistic duration   109, 110
over-assignment   131
overtalking   42

panicker   34
parallel working   157
percentage complete, 102
  focus on the past, 104
  graphical represenation, 103
  hides problems, 104
  How far to walk?, 104
PERT charts   212, 215
  advantages   218
  disadvantages   218
pessimistic duration   109, 110
predecessors   128–29, 134, 213
President John F Kennedy   63

PRINCE2
  closing a croject (CP)   224
  controlling a stage (CS)
      222
  directing a project (DP)   222
  initiating a project (IP)   221
  managing product delivery
      (MP)   223
  managing stage boundaries
      (SB)   223
  planning (PL)   222
  starting up a project
      (SU)   221
  strengths   224
  weaknesses   225
prioritizing issues   195
probability   139, 146
  risk   139
probably duration   110
problem solving
    techniques   229
  Fishbone diagrams   229
  The 'Five Whys'   231
project approaches   219
project board   171
project charter   48
  background   51
  budget   52
  contents   51
  creating   48
  milestones   51
  objectives   51
  risks   52
  timescales   51
  tolerances   52
project closure   203
project committee   171
project crashing   119, 160
project initialization   44
project initiation

objectives   47
project killers   9
    death by content   11
    doomed team   10
    'everything goes right'
        plans   12
    ignored team   9
    incompetent team   9
    relaxed team   11
    scared team   9
project management
    agreed objective   22
    agreeing objectives   57
    control   7
    customers   47
    description   7
    diagnostic   19
    evidence   10
    getting to the truth   19
    implementing   7
    initialization   44
    killing projects   13
    leading projects   33
    managing projects well   8
    organizing   7
    planning   7
    providing feedback   7
    responsibilities   167
    scope   44
Project Management Book of
    Knowledge   219
project management
    software   26, 85, 87, 103,
        113, 124, 129, 132, 135,
        155–56, 181–82, 211
    calendar function   117
    calendar view   118
    non-working time   119
    resource usage   155
project manager   7, 10–11, 14,

20, 24–27, 33–35, 37, 39,
    45–48, 50, 52, 59, 61, 70,
    86, 93, 98, 100–01, 108, 111,
    121–22, 124, 136, 139, 142,
    160, 167, 169, 170, 173, 175,
    181, 183–85, 194, 197–99,
    202–05, 207, 211–12, 221–23,
    225
project methodologies   219
project office   171
project plan   2, 22–24, 26, 38,
    131, 151–53, 169–70, 178,
    181–82, 198, 202, 212, 215
    integrating update
        information   179
    monitoring progress   184
    update form   179
    update information   178
    updating   178, 181
project review   203
project scope   44
project sponsor   115, 168, 170,
    171, 176, 199, 202, 203
project team
    trust   107
project team members   14, 122,
    167, 169, 178
project update form   179
projects
    What is a project?   5
    What is project
        management?   6

quality   7

race into space   63
refining milestones   76
relaxed team   11
reporting   201
    down   201

up   202
resource availability   114
resource commitments
   baseline hours   116
   understanding   115
resource managers   36, 104,
   157, 168, 204
resource usage   26, 131,
   152–53, 155, 221
resources   7
   assigning   96
   identifying   96
   improving resource
      usage   153
   over-assignment   131
   role types   97
result paths   76, 81
   assessing   79
   categories   77
   creating   78
   relationship   78
   setting up   77
result paths   83
risk   136
   assessment   139
   certain   138
   combination of risk and
      probabiliity   140
   composite score   142
   differences compared to
      issues   194
   example risk scoring   140
   identifying   137
   managing   137
   mapping   139
   optimization   158
   reduction   143
   time urgency   142
   uncertain   138
   weekly discussions   145

risk assessment   139
risk identification   138
risk management   136, 145
   contingency   143
risk reduction   143
   avoidance   143
   contingency   143
risk register   140
risk types   144
roles   167
   communication   172
   project manager   167
   project office   171
   project sponsor   170
   project team members   167,
      169
   steering group   171
   work package
      managers   169
rolling wave planning   90

scared project manager   14
scared team   9
Schedule Performance Indicator
   (SPI)   189
Schedule Variance (SV)   189
skyscraper construction   86
slack   107, 133, 135
SMART objectives   59
software package   155
specification   7
sponsor   47, 50
stage gate™ process   71
stakeholders   50
start to start   134
state of achievement   1, 51, 66,
   68, 70, 74
steering group   170–71, 199
subcontractor   157
sub-milestones   82

sub-tasks   94, 129–31, 213–14,
    216–17
successors   128–29, 134, 213
summary tasks   130
sunk costs   15
swim lanes   76

task duration, 152
  rule of thumb
        calculation   115
team issues   204
time estimation   100
time related risk   144
timescales   7
tolerances   52
toll gate   72
top level plans   167
total slack   133

unlimited resources   39
update information   178
updates   145, 167–68, 170, 179
updating the plan   178, 181
  frequency   182
US railway   205

Vegas project manager   14
video games   208

well defined milestones   66
well defined objectives   59
'What, Why, When, How,
        Where and Who'   61
work breakdown   51
work breakdown structure   82,
        86–87, 89, 93, 100, 129
  definition   86
  rolling wave planning   90
  task numbering   87
work packages   87
work content   101–02,
        106–109, 111–12, 114–15,
        121–22, 137, 152, 169,
        178–82
  definition   107
work package managers   169
work packages   51, 86–87, 93,
        169, 177, 222–23
working in parallel   157
working time   118
writing milestones   70